THE
MEANING AND MESSAGE
OF THE
BOOK OF REVELATION

THE
MEANING AND MESSAGE
OF THE
BOOK OF REVELATION

❊

EDWARD A. McDOWELL

Professor of New Testament Interpretation
Southeastern Baptist Theological Seminary
Wake Forest, N.C.

❊

Broadman Press

NASHVILLE, TENNESSEE

Printed in the United States of America

To Doris

For she herself also hath been a helper of many, and of mine own self.

—ROMANS 16:2

FOREWORD

IT is hardly necessary to say that no claim of infallibility is made for this interpretation of the book of Revelation. I am duly conscious of its limitations, and I am also aware of the fact that some of the conclusions drawn are open to question. But who can ever be certain of the answers to all the questions connected with the book of Revelation? Those who are most certain that their answers are correct are perhaps the interpreters least likely to be right. And yet there are many great truths in the book concerning which there need be no debate. I hope that the discussion of these truths in the pages that follow will compensate for the uncertainty that may be raised by the interpretation of obscure and difficult points.

There is always room for an interpretation of Revelation which takes into account its historic setting and at the same time seeks to make its teaching relevant to our own time. I hope that these two demands have been met in this treatment. The book of Revelation does contain a message for those of us who live in the dawn of the atomic age and who sincerely seek to make a vital interpretation of the gospel in a time of crisis and transition.

I am indebted to many helpers, some of them unknown to me personally, in the writing of this book. Those unknown to me personally are scholars whose books I have drawn upon and whose ideas have stimulated my thinking. The helpers known to me consist of my students, my colleagues, and my wife. Among students to whom I owe a debt of gratitude are those who were members of my seminar in the book of Revelation during the session of 1948–1949 at the Southern Baptist Theological Seminary. To Rev. Barney Freasier, my fellow in Greek New Testament, I am grateful for careful reading of the manuscript and checking of references. Dr.

Henry Turlington, my colleague in the Department of New Testament Interpretation, read the manuscript and made valuable suggestions. Dr. Dale Moody, another colleague on the faculty of the seminary, also read the manuscript and gave me encouragement. My wife, who is my helper in all things, read the manuscript and added her part to its improvement. Mrs. Elgin Lee, the typist, deserves much praise for her faithful work and her joy in serving. To all these I express my heartfelt appreciation.

I cannot forget that much of this volume was "tried out" first upon interested groups of ministers and laymen in several Bible conferences at various places over the South and that sympathetic hearers attending these conferences encouraged me to believe that a book on Revelation might be well received. I remember the encouragement of these friends, and I hope they will not be disappointed in this effort to interpret the most difficult of all the New Testament writings.

I have used the American Standard Version in quoting the Scripture text, but I have made my own translation of passages when a more faithful rendering of the original seemed necessary.

EDWARD A. MCDOWELL

Louisville, Kentucky

I am grateful for the reception that has been given this book. Since a new printing is necessary, I take this opportunity of expressing my gratitude for all of the messages of appreciation I have received concerning the book.

E. A. M.

Wake Forest, North Carolina
October, 1954.

ACKNOWLEDGMENTS

TO THE Macmillan Company, New York, for permission to use the quotations from *The Apocalypse of St. John,* Third Edition, by H. B. Swete, and the quotation from *The Apocalypse of John* by Isbon T. Beckwith.

To the Oxford University Press, New York, for permission to use the quotations from *The Apocrypha and Pseudepigrapha of the Old Testament,* Vol. II, by R. H. Charles.

To Charles Scribner's Sons, New York, for permission to use the quotation from *The Revelation of St. John* by R. H. Charles, in *The International Critical Commentary.*

To the International Council of Religious Education for permission to use Scripture quotations from the American Standard Edition of the Revised Bible, copyrighted 1901.

CONTENTS

The Great Drama of the Sovereignty of God

ACT ONE

ACT TWO

EPILOGUE

Chapter I

HOW REVELATION
CAME TO BE WRITTEN

IT is a strange book and, to many, a closed book, this book
that in our English Bibles appears under the title, "The
Revelation of St. John the Divine." But while it may
remain strange, it need not remain closed. If we cannot understand all of it, we can understand much of it. This is a
quest to understand as much of its meaning and message as
diligent study and guidance of the Spirit may make possible.

We must take the trouble to learn as much as possible
concerning the historical situation to which the book of Revelation belongs. It is only when this historical situation is
reconstructed that Revelation comes alive and we are able
to enter sympathetically into the mind and heart of the
author and his readers. Perhaps no other book of the Bible
has suffered more from being wrenched from its historical
context than has Revelation.

When Revelation is studied in its historical context, it becomes relevant for our own time. The book was written in a
period of crisis to help first-century Christians meet specific
problems arising out of this crisis. If we take the trouble to
learn the nature of this crisis, the book begins to speak to us
and to our own time. We are able to see behind the strange
symbols and the unfamiliar imagery the truths that had vital
meaning for the people who read the book in the first century.
We discover that in the ancient world of the book's origin
there were elements that are present in our own world, and

1

we are led to make applications of the great truths of the book to the conditions of our own time. Our adventure into the past enables us to see that the message spoken by the Holy Spirit in a given historical situation can be repeated, and repeated with emphasis. The lesson we learn is that the Holy Spirit does not contradict himself. The message he gave in the first century is valid in the twentieth century. But we learn that the message was given in the first instance through the medium of thought forms, conditions, and circumstances that prevailed in the first century. Hence to discover the message the Spirit gave at the first and to apply that message properly to our own situation demand that we inquire diligently into the historical situation and the thought forms that prevailed when the book was written. Only by fulfilling this demand can we conscientiously claim the leadership of the Spirit in interpreting the book in our own time. Let us therefore make the effort to reconstruct the historical context of the book of Revelation.

The Date of Writing

There is an unusual degree of unanimity among scholars in recent years as to the date of the writing of Revelation. The verdict of modern scholarship is that the book was written during the reign of Emperor Domitian, who ruled from A.D. 81 to 96. Other possible dates have been suggested, the most likely being a date during the reign of Nero (A.D. 54–68). The book undoubtedly reflects conditions which prevailed in Nero's time, as, for instance, the vivid description of the destruction of Rome by fire in chapter 18, the background of which must have been the actual burning of the city under Nero.

But there are several reasons for rejecting the Neronic date in favor of the Domitianic date. The first of these is that the persecution described in Revelation is more extensive than that which the Christians suffered under Nero. Under Nero the Christians were persecuted and suffered martyrdom in the city of Rome, but there is no evidence that the persecution extended into the provinces. The persecution described in Revelation had reached into the provinces (2:13) and had resulted in the martyrdom of Christians (2:13; 6:9; 20:4). The first persecution of Christians resulting from the policy of an emperor and extending into the provinces came under Domitian and toward the latter part of his reign. Two of Domitian's victims in Rome are known by name. They were T. Flavius Clemens, a cousin of the emperor, and Domitilla, this man's wife and a niece of Domitian. The former was put to death, while the latter was banished to an island off the coast of Campania. According to Dio Cassius, Flavius Clemens and his wife were charged with "atheism."[1] H. B. Swete says: "Putting the data together it is natural to infer that Fl. Clemens and his wife suffered for their Christian faith, and that they were by no means the only victims of Domitian's hostility to 'Jewish ways.' "[2] Swete also points out the fact that Melito, bishop of Sardis, in writing to the Emperor Antoninus (Eusebius, *Ecclesiastical History*, iv. 26), coupled the name of Domitian with that of Nero as a persecutor. Swete concludes that an Asian bishop would hardly have named Domitian along with Nero in this fashion unless the persecution under Domitian had extended beyond Rome.[3]

There is no evidence that Nerva and Trajan, the emperors who succeeded Domitian, continued his policy of persecution. The book of Revelation does not fit the conditions prevailing in their time, and it would be impossible to date it in the reigns of later emperors who conducted severe persecutions against Christians.

Another reason for fixing the time of the writing of the book in Domitian's reign rather than in Nero's is the apparent use by the author of the myth of Nero's resurrection. In the description of the beast in 13:3, one of the heads is said to have suffered a death stroke and been healed. This same

[1]*History of Rome*, lxvii. 14. 1f.
[2]*The Apocalypse of St. John*, p. lxxxv.
[3]*Ibid.*, p. lxxxvi.

3

beast is referred to again in 17:8 in this fashion: "The beast that thou sawest was, and is not; and is about to come up out of the abyss, and to go into perdition." There was a legend that arose after Nero's death to the effect that he would come from Parthia leading an army and re-establish himself as the head of the empire. Of course, the author of Revelation did not believe this myth, but it seems fairly certain that he has employed it in connection with his symbolism. This being true, his book must of necessity have been written after Nero's time.

(3) Yet another reason for accepting the Domitianic date is the state of the churches as revealed in the seven letters. Apparently these churches have been in existence for several generations, certainly long enough since their founding around the middle of the century to allow for the cooling of the ardor characteristic of new churches and for the entrance of heresies into some of them.

We conclude that the internal evidence of Revelation argues for its writing in the reign of Domitian.

The external evidence is also on the side of the later date. Irenaeus, the church father, in his work *Against the Heresies,* written between A.D. 181 and 189, places the time of writing in Domitian's reign. Eusebius, the great church historian of the fourth century, and Jerome, who was born in A.D. 346, great Bible scholar who gave the version of the Bible known as the *Vulgate* to the world, say that Revelation was written during Domitian's time.

The persecution instituted under Domitian came at the latter part of his reign. We therefore date the book A.D. 95–96.

The Purpose

The purpose of Revelation is closely related to the policy of Domitian in insisting that his subjects worship him as a god. It was nothing new for an emperor to encourage the belief that he was divine. The cult of emperor worship was established in the early days of the empire. Such names as

4

"god" (Greek, *theos*) and "savior" (*sotēr*) were commonly applied to the emperors. Julius Caesar had his statue placed among the images of the gods in the temples. Augustus (27 B.C. to A.D. 14) accepted from the senate the title "Augustus" (*sebastos*), a title ordinarily applied to the gods. Caius Caligula (A.D. 37–41) demanded universal homage to his statue. His effort to set up his statue in the Temple at Jerusalem was fiercely resisted by the Jews, and because of this resistance he desisted from his purpose. A second effort to carry out his intention was cut short by his death. No emperor until Domitian carried out a policy of compulsion implemented by persecution. Not even the terrible Nero had such a policy. "He shrank from the title *Divus* and the erection of temples in his honor."[4] Not so with Domitian: "No such feelings held back Domitian from pressing his claims to Divine honours. He found a gloomy and perhaps a cynical pleasure in the shouts which greeted his arrival at the amphitheatre with Domitia; *domino et dominae feliciter.* Unable to rouse enthusiasm or admiration, he could insist on being regarded as a god."[5]

Perhaps there was no division of the empire which more readily fell in with Domitian's policy than the province of Asia. The province was proud of her membership in the empire and seized upon every occasion to magnify her relation to it. She delighted in honoring the emperors, as her many inscriptions lauding them testify, and as the honor she did to their statues proves. The cult of Caesar worship was very popular in Asia. Asia was fertile ground for cults and mysteries of all kinds, and none was more welcome than this cult which combined so adroitly patriotism, religion, and mysticism. Once the provincial officials of the emperor cult understood the seriousness with which Domitian regarded his claim to divinity, they would rush to the execution of his policy. And it was at this point that the Christian communities of the province of Asia ran afoul of the imperial Roman power. They were faced with the dilemma of obeying the policy of

[4]Swete, *op. cit.*, p. lxxxviii.
[5]*Ibid.*, p. lxxxviii. Swete's authority for the statement is Suetonius, *Dom.* 13.

the Caesar and disowning supreme allegiance to Christ or of refusing to pay divine honors to the emperor and thereby inviting the penalty of ostracism, exile, torture, imprisonment, or death. The Christians might prove their patriotism and loyalty to the emperor by making an offering before his statue and saying the words *Kyrios Kaisar* ("Lord Caesar"). It was a simple procedure, but it involved the basic loyalty of Christians to God and to Christ. In his insistence upon this evidence of loyalty, the secular ruler had chosen to invade the sanctity of the individual's deepest experiences with God; by it he blasphemously claimed the right to dethrone God as revealed in Jesus Christ. To maintain the integrity of his relationship with God and of his Christian experience, there was no way open to the individual Christian but to reject obedience to this blasphemous ritual which would elevate Caesar above Christ. His duty was clear—he could only say, *Kurios Iēsous* ("Lord Jesus").

There is no evidence that a great flame of persecution burst upon the Christian communities as a result of their resistance to the policy of Domitian. But resistance was met inevitably with arrest and persecution of Christians. As the persecution gained quiet momentum, it caught in its progress one of the leaders of the Asian churches. His lot was banishment to a little island called Patmos, located off the coast of Asia. There he had opportunity to meditate upon the meaning of the conflict that had arisen between the Roman state and the Christian church. He saw the conflict in its historical and cosmic significance; and as he brooded upon its vast implications, he fell into an ecstasy, and there came to him under the inspiration of the Holy Spirit the vision, or visions, that were written down in the book we call Revelation.

The Seer of Patmos recognized the irreconcilable nature of the rising conflict between Rome and Christianity. He realized that it was a battle to the death. He saw that two sovereignties, each claiming absolute allegiance, could not exist side by side. Christ or Caesar must win in the struggle. In the meantime Christians were dying in the conflict, and others would suffer and lose their lives because of their loyalty to the gospel. The conflict would grow in intensity until it was settled in some great clash of opposing forces. The churches must gird themselves for the crisis. But were they ready? Would the quality of their life bear the strain of the impending struggle? Other questions pressed for answers in the mind of the Seer. Why were God's people allowed to suffer? How long would their blood go unavenged? Was God upon his throne exercising control over history? Did he care for his people? How would deliverance come? The Christians of Asia and perhaps throughout the empire would desire answers to these questions; they would need encouragement and assurance, if these could honestly be given.

The answer to these questions came to John on his lonely island in the form of visions that were wrought into a book. Addressed to the "seven churches of Asia," the writing was doubtless intended for reading by all the churches of Asia and perhaps of the empire. The book was sent out as Christianity's answer to the challenge of the Caesars. Its message was one of encouragement and hope and of ultimate victory for those who were loyal to Christ. No doubt the message fired many an anxious Christian heart with holy zeal for the gospel and made him ready to die in the cause, if death was to be the price of his loyalty.

The Character of the Book

The book of Revelation belongs to a particular type of literature which was popular in Palestine in the last two centuries before Christ and in the first century of the Christian Era. Books belonging to this type of literature have been called "tracts for hard times" because they were written, for the most part, in times of distress to give encouragement to oppressed and persecuted people. These writings are designated "apocalyptic literature," the word "apocalyptic" being taken from the Greek word *apokalupsis* in the first verse of Revelation where it is translated "Revelation"—"The Revela-

7

tion of Jesus Christ." The verb form of the word *apokaluptō* means to unveil. Revelation being the greatest of all the apocalypses, the word was taken from its title to designate all the apocalyptic literature.

Daniel was the great apocalypse that set the pattern for most of the writings of apocalyptic nature that follow. Revelation reflects much of the imagery and style of Daniel. There are portions of other Old Testament books that belong to the apocalyptic type, notably Isaiah 13–14, Ezekiel 1 and 28–39, Joel 2–3, and Zechariah 9–14. The author of Revelation was strongly influenced in the choice of symbols and somewhat in the use of ideas by Ezekiel.

Outside the Old Testament there was a large number of books of the apocalyptic type widely circulated among the Jews. The most important of these were the following: Ethiopic *Enoch,* the oldest portions of which were written before 160 B.C., the latest before 64 B.C.; Slavonic *Enoch,* which belongs probably to the first century; the *Sibylline Oracles,* books III–V, not later than second century B.C.; the *Psalms of Solomon,* written soon after Pompey captured Jerusalem in 63 B.C.; the *Odes of Solomon,* dated by Harnack between 50 B.C. and A.D. 67; the *Testaments of the Twelve Patriarchs,* the oldest portions belonging to the second century B.C., the youngest portions to the first half of the first century A.D.; the *Book of Jubilees,* written near the beginning of the first century; *Second Esdras,* belonging to the *Apocrypha* and written in the latter part of the first century A.D.; the *Apocalypse of Baruch,* belonging to the latter part of the first century A.D.; the *Assumption of Moses,* written in the early part of the first century A.D. (Jude in the New Testament draws from this book in discussing the dispute between Michael and the devil about the body of Moses.)

What are the characteristics of these apocalyptic writings? First of all, they emphasize eschatological hopes and expectations; that is to say, they stress the hopes and expectations of the people of God concerning last things, or the consummation of history. They give assurance of God's intervention

8

for the deliverance of his people. Present struggles and problems are depicted against the background of the end of history.

The messages of the apocalyptic writings, for the most part, are set in a framework of visions and raptures experienced by the authors. These visions are often depicted in a series of extraordinary symbols. Strange creatures, animals and birds of almost unimaginable character, are employed to convey the author's ideas. Ezekiel's four living creatures and wheels, and the four living creatures and beasts of Revelation are illustrations.

There can be no doubt that the author of Revelation was influenced by other apocalyptic writings in his style and choice of symbols, but a comparison of his work with these other writings will show that he exercised the independence of a genius in the use of them. He was no slavish copyist. His work stands out as far superior to all the other apocalypses in organization, in ideas, and in use of symbols.

In the case of the Revelation, it is most likely that much of the symbolism used was more than a matter of style. Many of the symbols were doubtless employed to conceal ideas that would have caused trouble for the readers of the book had they become known to the Roman authorities. The Apocalypse plainly predicted the downfall of Rome and the victory of Christ over the Caesars. Thus it was a piece of seditious literature. The truths of a seditious nature which the book conveyed might safely be hidden under strange symbols, understandable to the Christian readers but unintelligible to the Roman authorities.

The Apocalypse of John is superior to the other apocalypses in its organization. Where many of the apocalypses are disjointed, the Revelation is orderly. It moves with the precision and beauty of a great pageant; indeed, it has many of the characteristics of a modern pageant. It also possesses the majesty and feeling of a great drama or a great poem. Its poetic and dramatic qualities are everywhere in evidence.

The marked superiority of Revelation over other apoca-

9

lypses is in its message, and this it derives from the Christian gospel. It is this message with its great ideas of redemption, of the sovereignty of God, of judgment, of the vindication of God, and of righteousness in history that has been clothed with the strange vestments of symbolism, pageantry, and apocalyptic. It is this message which more than anything else lifts the Apocalypse above all other writings of its class and makes it the superior of them all.

There is another difference between Revelation and other apocalypses that should be noted. Almost without exception the apocalyptic writings are represented as being written by ancient worthies who could not have been their authors. These writings which were circulated under the names of men who were not their authors have been classified as "pseudonymous"; that is, as using a false name. The non-canonical books written under the names of Moses, Enoch, Baruch, and Ezra are works of this class. But here the Revelation parts company again with the other apocalypses. The author makes no effort to hide his identity; indeed, he takes pains to identify himself. He is obviously a person who is well known to the churches of Asia and one whose name carries authority. It is clear that he does not seek to gain a hearing for his writing by "putting himself off" as the apostle John. If he is the apostle John, he makes no unnatural and belabored claims to prove his apostleship. If he is not the apostle John, he sends forth his writing under his own name with the straightforward claim to be who he is, a person well known to his readers. He says: "I John, your brother and partaker with you in the tribulation and kingdom and patience which are in Jesus, was in the isle that is called Patmos, for the word of God and the testimony of Jesus" (1:9).

It should be remembered that the Revelation is a *prophetic* work as well as an apocalypse. The author claims to be a prophet, as we have seen. But our author is more than a prophet in the common New Testament sense; he is a *writing* prophet. His work is the only New Testament prophetic book. Thus the author of the Apocalypse has the distinction of re-

10

viving the biblical office of writing prophet. He is doubtless fully conscious of this role. No other New Testament writer seems to be so clearly aware as our author that he is writing Scripture. This is evident from his warning in 22:18 f.: "I testify unto every man that heareth the words of the prophecy of this book, If any man shall add unto them, God shall add unto him the plagues which are written in this book: and if any man shall take away from the words of the book of this prophecy, God shall take away his part from the tree of life, and out of the holy city, which are written in this book."

The Author

We have seen that the author makes no effort to conceal his identity under a pseudonym. He plainly identifies himself as John. But what John was he? The traditional view is that he was John the son of Zebedee, member of the twelve. The testimony of the church fathers is heavily on the side of this view. Justin Martyr, who lived at Ephesus before the generation that received the Apocalypse passed away, in his *Dialogue Against Trypho* (81), refers to Revelation as an acknowledged work of John the apostle. Irenaeus, younger contemporary of Justin, in the latter half of the second century, speaks of the Apocalypse as that of "John the disciple of the Lord" (iii. 11. 1 ff., iv. 20. 11). Clement of Alexandria, Tertullian, Origen, and the Muratorian Canon all testify to the Johannine authorship.

The author seems to have been a Palestinian Jew, which John the son of Zebedee was. The book is certainly strongly colored by Hebrew thought and language. The language is hardly that which would have been used by a Greek or cultured Roman citizen. Apparently the author thought in Hebrew or Aramaic. R. H. Charles thinks that the Greek, while unlike any "that was ever penned by mortal man," follows certain rules of the author's own invention, indicating that he never really mastered the commonly spoken Greek of his own

11

time and that he acquired what Greek he knew late in life. Charles also believes that the author was a native of Galilee, because he claimed to be a prophet (22:9) and because he was a master of apocalyptic literature.[6]

The problem of the authorship of the Revelation is tied up with that of the authorship of the Gospel of John and the Epistles of John. It is a complex problem and is too involved for elaborate discussion in this book. There is a strong bond of kinship in ideas between the Gospel and the Apocalypse. This does not appear on the surface because of the marked difference in purpose, language, and style in the two books. And yet the great fundamental ideas concerning God, Christ, redemption, and sin are present in both books. In Revelation they are clothed in apocalyptic language, but they are the same great ideas that appear in different form in the Gospel of John. This suggests that at Ephesus in the latter part of the first century, there was developed a school of thought out of which came the "Johannine" literature, all of which bore the stamp of one great mind. A school called the "Ephesian School" is thought by several scholars to have existed. What is more reasonable than to think that the apostle John, living in Ephesus in his latter days, was the person whose mind left its indelible stamp upon the Ephesian Christian community and whose interpretation of the gospel was the core of teaching upon which the "Ephesian School" was founded? If we accept this view, there is no difficulty in identifying the "beloved disciple" of the Gospel of John with the apostle. By this view it is reasonable to identify John the apostle as the author of the Fourth Gospel and at the same time allow for collaboration and assistance he may have received from leaders in the Christian community at Ephesus.

But there is sufficient warrant for raising the question as to whether the John of Revelation is to be identified with John the apostle. He does not claim to be the apostle, and

[6]*The Revelation of St. John,* "International Critical Commentary," Vol. I, pp. xxi and cxliii f.

HOW REVELATION CAME TO BE WRITTEN

in no place does he attempt to identify himself as the apostle. The author of the Gospel is identified as the "disciple whom Jesus loved" (John 21:20,24); and the "disciple whom Jesus loved" is identified as one of the twelve (13:23; 19:26; 20:2). The author of Revelation represents himself as being a prophet (10:11; 22:9).

There is a tradition concerning another John at Ephesus. Eusebius, the church historian, says in his *Ecclesiastical History* (iii, 39. 6): "There were two tombs in Ephesus, both of which bear the name of John even to this day." Eusebius goes on to identify one of these Johns with "the Elder John" mentioned by Papias in his famous fragment preserved by Eusebius. Eusebius says that it was probably this Elder John who "saw the Apocalypse bearing the name of John" (iii, 39. 6).

It is possible, but by no means certain, that Eusebius is correct in identifying the author of Revelation with this Elder John. If he is the author, he was likely the author of the Second and Third Epistles of John, for the author of these little letters calls himself "the Elder." But the First Epistle of John was most certainly written by the same man who wrote the Gospel.

There is yet the possibility that the author of Revelation was neither the apostle nor the Elder John but another John who was well known to the churches of Asia. Whoever he may have been, he was undoubtedly strongly influenced by the "Ephesian School" of thought. If John the apostle was the father of this school, as has been suggested, the author of the Apocalypse was the heir of the thinking and spirit of the son of Zebedee, and the mind of the beloved disciple is in Revelation as well as in the Gospel which bears his name.

Whoever this John who wrote Revelation was, he was a man of genius, one of the greatest of all the seers. He ranks with the great religious geniuses of the ages. Like Saul of Tarsus, he was called to a great task at a critical time in the life of Christianity. He did not fail in the discharge of his stewardship. The Holy Spirit gave through his mind and

13

heart one of the greatest of all religious works. The proof of the genius and power of the author is the influence of Revelation in spite of the difficulties that surround its interpretation and the violence to which it has been subjected by interpreters through the centuries.

Chapter II

HOW THE DRAMA OF REVELATION
IS UNFOLDED

THE book of Revelation tells a dramatic story of a conflict in sovereignty between the sovereignty of God asserted in history through Jesus Christ and the pretended sovereignty of Satan asserted in history through the imperial Roman power. The conflict is resolved with the utter overthrow of Satan and the complete victory of God through his agent, Jesus Christ.

Preceding the actual drama or pageant of this cosmic conflict are: the title and superscription (1:1–3), the address and salutation (1:4–8), the opening vision and the author's commission to write (1:9–20), and the letters to the seven churches (chaps. 2–3).

These seven were actual churches. There were many other churches in the empire; these are representative of them all. Each letter was intended for all the churches, and all the letters were intended for each church. Ramsay suggests that each of the cities named was a postal center and that from each of these centers the Apocalypse was sent out to surrounding churches. The letters reveal the author's deep concern for the spiritual vitality of the churches in the face of impending persecution. Sin and heresy had found their way into the churches, and this brought forth stern words of rebuke and ringing challenges to holier living. In the letters the reader may find the majestic person of the exalted Christ in a sevenfold manifestation. He may also discover a sevenfold representation of reward promised to those that are faithful to Christ and his cause.

The dramatic pageant of the book's action actually opens with the great vision of the Court of Heaven in the fourth and fifth chapters. God is pictured in exalted majesty upon the throne of the universe. His sovereignty is emphasized in the worship rendered him by the four and twenty elders, each of whom is a king. The scroll in the hand of God, which no one could open, contains revelations of some of the great problems of history. Only the Lamb, who is also the Lion of the tribe of Judah, is worthy to break the seals and reveal these problems and set them in their proper relationship to the gospel and the purposes of God.

The first six seals are broken in quick succession. Their revelations may be called "History's Pageant of Suffering": (1) conquest, (2) war, (3) famine, (4) death, (5) the death of God's people, (6) the end of history. The "Great Interlude" of chapter seven follows. It depicts the redemption of God's people on the earth (1–8) and the eternal salvation of God's people in heaven (9–17).

Another series of seven is begun at this point: the seven trumpet angels. The great series of plagues under the trumpeting of the first six angels (chaps. 8–9) may be called "The Tragedy of Unrepenting Humanity." They show the obstinacy of man in his unregenerate state in spite of the operation of the wrath of God.

The "interlude" of chapters 10 and 11 is exceedingly important because it points to the heart of the message of the Apocalypse in 11:15. This, it will be noted, is given under the seventh trumpet blast following the breaking of the seventh seal. By this device the author endeavors to mark very plainly the sum and substance of the whole matter, namely,

The sovereignty (basileia) *over the world, became* (egeneto) *our Lord's and his Christ's and he shall reign forever and ever.*

16

From this point on to the description of the judgment (20:11–15) the story is that of the conflict of sovereignties: the sovereignty of God manifested in Jesus Christ and the sovereignty asserted by Satan through evil world powers. The action moves on to the complete overthrow of the evil world powers (19:19–21), with the accompanying limitation of the power of Satan (20:1–3), and finally the utter defeat of Satan himself (20:10).

It is significant that the great declaration of the sovereignty of God in 11:15 is followed almost immediately in chapter 12 by the description of the birth of the Messiah. The casting down of Satan from heaven is the author's way of describing the great defeat suffered by Satan when Christ's work on earth was completed. The victory in heaven, however, precipitates a great conflict on earth, for immediately Satan incites the beast that arises out of the sea to make war with the followers of Christ (chap. 13). The beast symbolizes the succession of emperors or the imperial power. He is also the incarnation of evil at its worst—evil as witnessed in Nero, since the wounded and restored head likely symbolizes Nero. Hence the first beast is Antichrist. The second beast (13:11) symbolizes the officials of the emperor cult who were charged with enforcing the decree of the emperor that he should be paid divine honors.

Chapter 14 contains another of the interesting "interludes" of the book. It gives a series of seven assurances and warnings in connection with the great impending conflict. Another series of seven follows. It is a description of the pouring out of the bowls of God's wrath. The pouring out of these bowls represents the wrath of God as it is manifested in all its power against the evil world powers that set themselves against his sovereignty. The pouring out of the seventh bowl introduces the action culminating in the destruction of Babylon, which is Rome, the center of the imperial power and seat of Antichrist's rule. The judgment and fall of Rome are dramatically portrayed in the sevenfold series in 17:1 to 19:5.

The victory of Christ and his followers over the beast and

17

his allies is now described (19:6-21). Christ wins by the power of a sword which proceeds from his mouth (19:15,21). His name is "the Word of God" (19:13); he is "King of kings, and Lord of lords" (19:16). All this is intended to convey the assurance of a great spiritual victory which the author sees as the outcome of the impending struggle between Christ and Caesar. This victory is to take place within history: *Christianity will survive the assaults of the imperial Roman power.*

The binding of Satan (20:1-3) for a thousand years represents the cosmic result of the defeat of Satan in history. The defeat of the beast and his allies is a defeat for Satan and signalizes the limitation of his power for a long, indeterminate period of time (1,000 years). The reign of the martyrs and saints begins in this period of struggle. Those who are faithful to Christ in this struggle go from this earth at their death to reign with Christ for a long, indeterminate period of time (1,000 years): "This is the first resurrection" (20:4-6). But history continues even as the martyrs reign with Christ. Nevertheless the author grappled with the problem of the end of history. Satan's power would be limited, but so long as history lasted he could not be completely overthrown. The final end of Satan's power would come at the end of history; and this the author prophesied (20:10). But this would be preceded by one last great conflict in history, between Christ and Satan (20:1-9). The end of history and of Satan's power is cataclysmic and is initiated in heaven (20:9).

The final defeat of Satan and the end of history are followed by the judgment and the abolition of death (20:11-15). Above and beyond history are the new heaven and the new earth and the new Jerusalem (21:1 to 22:5). The new Jerusalem does not arise out of history but comes "down out of heaven from God" (21:2). In this beautiful section the author seeks to portray with marvelous imagery the blessed supernatural, suprahistorical life which awaits the people of God. The new Jerusalem is the perfect city. It is described as having seven great attributes of perfection (21:9 to 22:5).

18

The conclusion of the book (22:6–21) contains a validation of the vision (6–9), a warning to heed the message of the book (10–20), and the benediction (21).

The Plan of the Book

The book of Revelation is both pageant and drama. At times it is more like a pageant in that the action consists of a succession of visions without plot; but if the action of the book as a whole is held in view, it may be seen readily how the Apocalypse may be conceived of as a great drama. There are certainly two acts, if the main part of the book be treated as a drama. The subdivisions of the action may be conveniently divided into "scenes," as in the following scheme. Study of the book and its action will show that the action in each scene indicated below is justifiably conceived of as a unit. This is not to suggest that the author followed such a scheme in the writing of his book. It is obvious, however, that he followed an orderly arrangement and that there is progress in the action toward the grand climax. The following scheme will enable the reader to visualize the book as a whole and will provide a working plan for the exposition to follow.

THE GREAT DRAMA OF THE SOVEREIGNTY OF GOD

Introduction to the Great Drama.—Chapters 1–3
I. THE AUTHOR GIVES HIS CREDENTIALS AND PURPOSE.—Chapter 1
  1. A revelation that came from Jesus Christ (1:1–3)
  2. A revelation for the churches (1:4–8)
  3. The author's commission to write (1:9–20)
II. LETTERS TO THE SEVEN CHURCHES.—Chapters 2–3
  1. Ephesus: the church that left its first love (2:1–7)
  2. Smyrna: the rich poor church (2:8–11)
  3. Pergamum: the church that was close to Satan's throne (2:12–17)

4. Thyatira: the church that harbored a Jezebel (2:18–29)
5. Sardis: the church that had a name to live but was dead (3:1–6)
6. Philadelphia: the church with a door of opportunity set before it (3:7–13)
7. Laodicea: the church that was neither cold nor hot (3:14–22)

ACT ONE

God Asserts His Sovereignty over the World in Jesus Christ: The Court of Heaven and the Breaking of the Seven Seals.—Chapters 4–11

SCENE ONE: The Vision of the Court of Heaven. Chapters 4–5
1. The throne of God, the four and twenty elders, and the four living creatures (chap. 4)
2. The roll of the seven seals and acceptance by the Lamb of challenge to open it (chap. 5)

SCENE TWO: The Breaking of the Six Seals: *History's Pageant of Suffering.*—Chapter 6
1. The first four seals: the Four Horsemen—(1) conquest, (2) war, (3) famine, (4) death (6:1–6)
2. Fifth seal: the martyrs, or the suffering and death of the righteous (6:9–11)
3. Sixth seal: the end of the age (6:12–17)

SCENE THREE: Prelude to the Breaking of the Seventh Seal.—Chapter 7
1. The sealing of the servants of God (7:1–8)
2. A vision of the future blessedness of the redeemed (7:9–17)

SCENE FOUR: The Breaking of the Seventh Seal.—Chapters 8–9
1. Breaking of the seal and preparation of the seven trumpet angels (8:1–6)
2. The sounding of the six trumpets: *The Tragedy of Unrepenting Humanity* (8:7 to 9:21)
   (1) First four trumpets: doom of the third part of the material universe announced (8:7–12)

(2) Warning of the flying eagle (8:13)

(3) Fifth trumpet and end of first woe: the plague of fiendish locusts (9:1–12)

(4) Sixth trumpet: the plague of fiendish horses (9:13–21)

SCENE FIVE: The Prophet and the Eating of the Little Book in the Hand of the Great Angel.—Chapter 10

SCENE SIX: The Measuring of the Temple, the Two Prophets, the Great Earthquake, and the End of the Second Woe.—Chapter 11:1–14

SCENE SEVEN: The Sounding of the Seventh Trumpet: Proclamation of God's Sovereignty over the World. Chapter 11:15–19

ACT TWO

The Conflict of Sovereignties and the Victory of God: Messiah's Birth and Victory over Satan, the New Heaven and the New Earth, and the New Jerusalem.—Chapters 12:1 to 22:5

SCENE ONE: Messiah's Birth and Escape from the Dragon Satan, the Fall of Satan and His Angels, the Persecution of the Woman and Her Seed by the Dragon.—Chapter 12:1–17

SCENE TWO: Satan Continues His Warfare Against Christ Through Two Beasts.—Chapter 13

1. The first beast (the emperors) is given authority by the dragon (Satan) to persecute the saints (13:1–10)

2. The second beast (officials of the emperor cult) compels men to worship the first beast (13:11–18)

SCENE THREE: Seven Assurances and Warnings for the Great Conflict Between Christ and Satan.—Chapter 14

SCENE FOUR: Vision of the Seven Angels with the Bowls of the Wrath of God.—Chapters 15–16

1. Preparation in heaven for the pouring out of the bowls (chap. 15)

2. Pouring out of the bowls (chap. 16)

21

SCENE FIVE: Judgment of Babylon (Rome) and Proclamation of Her Doom.—Chapters 17:1 to 19:5
1. Vision and interpretation of the great harlot (chap. 17)
2. Sevenfold proclamation of judgment upon the great harlot (Babylon) (18:1 to 19:5)

SCENE SIX: The Victory of Christ over Satan and the Beast.—Chapters 19:6 to 20:6
1. Announcement of the marriage supper of the Lamb (19:6–10)
2. Appearance of Christ for the battle as King of kings and Lord of lords (19:11–16)
3. Invitation to the great supper of God and defeat of the beast and his allies (19:17–21)
4. The binding of Satan (20:1–3)
5. The reign of the martyrs and saints, and the first resurrection (20:4–6)
6. The final defeat of Satan (20:7–10)

SCENE SEVEN: The Judgment, the New Heaven and the New Earth, and the New Jerusalem.—Chapters 20:11 to 22:5
1. The resurrection, the judgment, and the end of death (20:11–15)
2. Introduction to the coming age (21:1–8)
3. The new Jerusalem: the perfect city (21:9 to 22:5)

EPILOGUE—*Conclusion of the Book.*—Chapter 22:6–21
1. Validation of the vision (6–9)
2. Warning to heed the message of the book (10–20)
3. Benediction (21)

Chapter III

THE AUTHOR GIVES
HIS CREDENTIALS AND PURPOSE

A Revelation That Came from Jesus Christ.—1:1-3

THE book we now begin to explore in detail is called by its author "a revelation of Jesus Christ." By this the author means that it is a revelation that came from Jesus Christ. The word for "revelation" is *apokalupsis*, which means an unveiling. The implication of the term is that the message given was designed to be understood. To many the book of Revelation is a closed book, impossible of understanding. It is comforting to discover at the very beginning that it was not written as a mystery to be hidden forever from the eyes of believers but as a book of help and comfort to be read and understood, not only by a few who were initiated into the meaning of its strange symbolism, but by all believers.

There is a pronouncement of blessing upon the reader and those who hear "the words of the prophecy, and keep the things that are therein." The author visualizes his book being read to a church assembled in public meeting. There is a suggestion in this of the urgency of the book's message and the purpose of the author to circulate it quickly among the churches. In his mind's eye he sees the congregations assembled and a reader standing before each group, while the hearers listen eagerly for every word as it comes from the reader's lips. The author is constrained by the importance of his message, and he is eager to share with the churches the revelation he has received. Doubtless he expected copies to be made of the roll he had written so that each of the seven churches might retain one. It is probable also that his intention was that yet other copies should be made available for churches located in the vicinity of each of the seven churches. John expected the fulfilment of many of the prophecies of his book at an early date, that is to say, in his own time. This is indicated by his statement that the revelation he received had to do with "the things which must shortly come to pass." This emphasizes the *historical* nature of much that is in Revelation and should give pause to the efforts of those interpreters who see in the prophetic elements of the book reference only to things that are yet to come to pass.

Further emphasis upon the fact that John expected the early fulfilment of many of his prophecies is seen in his statement, "The time is at hand." This statement should not be considered apart from its immediate context; it is not a reference to the second advent of Christ. The author means that the time is near, or, as the Greek says, "the season is near," for the fulfilment of the prophecies of the book. "Blessed is he that readeth," he says, "and they that hear the words of the prophecy, and keep the things that are therein: for the time is at hand."

These opening sentences contain another warning that modern interpreters would do well to heed. It is that the message of the book is clothed in symbols. Concerning the revelation, the author says, "He [Jesus Christ] sent and signified it by his angel unto his servant John." The Greek word for "signify" is *sēmaino*, which is made from the noun *sēma*, which means "a sign." That which is "signified" is indicated by some sort of sign. The author implies that the message he has received is being given to his readers under signs or symbols. Attention to this fact should save us from crass literalism in interpreting the message of the book. The author not only indicates here at the beginning that his message is given in symbols, but he repeatedly states as he unfolds his message that he is describing what he saw in visions. Now it is true that much of the revelation John received deals with

24

actual historical personalities and events, but the symbols and the visions are not to be interpreted as literal descriptions of these personalities and events. For instance, in the great vision of the Court of Heaven in chapters 4 and 5, Christ is represented as a lion and as a lamb. Common sense tells us that our Lord is not to be conceived of as actually taking the form of a lion or a lamb. But there are great spiritual truths concerning Christ that are taught by the use of these symbols. And so it is throughout the book.

The problem for any interpreter of Revelation is, of course, to interpret honestly and intelligently the symbols of the book. Honest and intelligent interpretation demands diligent study of the historical situation and of the Old Testament and apocalyptic backgrounds of the symbolism used. Even after this is done, one cannot be dogmatic in his conclusions; he must be willing to admit that there are mysteries about this book which the modern interpreter can never satisfactorily clarify.

A Revelation for the Churches.—1:4-8

The book of Revelation is rooted in a historical situation. This is emphasized by the address: "John to the seven churches that are in Asia." John's message is directed to the specific needs of a group of churches that had actual existence in the first century. This should warn the modern interpreter of the peril of disregarding the historical relationships of the book.

There is a magnificent ascription of praise in the address to the Father, the Holy Spirit, and the Son. Thus at the very beginning of the book we find the doctrine of the Trinity. The Holy Spirit appears under the apocalyptic appellation, "the seven Spirits that are before his throne." It is this reference to the Holy Spirit as "the seven Spirits" which enables us to identify the "seven Spirits of God" in 4:5 as the Holy Spirit, for it is clear that the Holy Spirit as a member of the Trinity is the subject of the author's allusion in the present passage. The number seven, which occurs so often in the book, is a symbol of completeness or perfection. The Holy Spirit is conceived of as the *perfect* Spirit, the Spirit capable of perfect representation of God.

God is presented here as the *Eternal* in a most remarkable way. He is described as the One who *is*, who *was*, and who *is to come*. The present participle of the verb "to be" is used to identify him as the God who *is*. He is, according to the Greek, the one being—*ho ōn*. No expression in the Greek language could more picturesquely suggest the limitless eternity of God's nature. God is also described as the One "who was." Here the Greek term is unique, one that only the author of Revelation would employ. It is the imperfect indicative active of the verb "to be," before which is placed the definite article: *ho ēn*. To suggest the limitless future existence of God, the author uses the present participle of the verb "to come" with the definite article: *hō erchomenos*.

We meet here with the exalted conception of Jesus Christ that is to be found throughout the book. In naming him "the faithful witness," the author doubtless conceives of his fidelity as a witness as being proved by his victory in death, for in the following statement he is described as "the firstborn of the dead." Our Lord, in the view of John, was the first martyr (Greek, *martus*) in that he sealed his testimony by his death and won victory over death through his resurrection. That he is the "firstborn of the dead" implies that he is the first and foremost of many who are to win the victory over death by rising from the dead. Here we meet with the first assertion of Christ's lordship over all earthly potentates. Later in the book he will appear as "King of kings, and Lord of lords" (19:16). Here he is just as truly represented as King of kings and Lord of lords, for he is described as "the ruler of the kings of the earth." It should be observed that the author thinks of Christ as possessing this lordship *now*. Certainly this assertion of the sovereignty of Jesus Christ cannot be referred to the future when he returns in his second advent. In the mind of the author he is King and sovereign *now*.

The statement, "He made us a kingdom, priests unto his God and Father," reflects the promise of Jehovah to the Israelites, "And ye shall be unto me a kingdom of priests, and a holy nation" (Exodus 19:6). (The Septuagint renders the Hebrew "a royal priesthood.") The meaning of the author of Revelation is that Christians have been constituted through the work of Christ a nation which fulfils the function assigned to ancient Israel, namely, the function of representing the human race to God. As the representative of the race before God, the new Israel, the body of Christians in the world, bears a sovereign character which makes it unique among the nations and gives to it the pre-eminence over all nations.

From its earliest days the Christian church was taught to expect the return of Jesus. The expectancy of his return is stated in verse 7: "Behold, he cometh with the clouds; and every eye shall see him, and they that pierced him; and all the tribes of the earth shall mourn over him." The verse reflects statements contained in Daniel 7:13 (with which should be put Mark 14:62) and Zechariah 12:10, 12, and 14. By the combination of these passages as a background, Jesus is interpreted as the great exalted Son of man who sits at the right hand of God ever ready to return in power and glory and at the same time as the Servant of Jehovah who suffered and died for his people. Daniel tells how "there came with the clouds of heaven one like unto a son of man." In response to the question of the high priest, "Art thou the Christ, the Son of the Blessed?" (Mark 14:61), Jesus said, "I am: and ye shall see the Son of man sitting at the right hand of Power, and coming with the clouds of heaven." In this declaration Jesus identifies himself as the great Danielic Son of man. He does not emphasize here his humanity but his power and glory as the supernatural representative of God. The combination of the expressions "sitting" and "coming" to describe the work of the great Son of man should not be overlooked. The meaning is that the Son of man, while occupying his appointed place of authority at the right hand of God, continues in the attitude of instant readiness to return to earth in glory. Now

27

the author of the Apocalypse, in a faithful portrayal of the picture of Christ in the Gospels has in this passage artistically combined the exalted Son of man with the Suffering Servant of Jehovah. Interpreting the passages from Zechariah as applying to the Messiah, he speaks of them "that pierced him" and of "all the tribes of the earth" mourning over him. The prophecy of Zechariah is interpreted as applying to the crucified Christ.

This reference to the return of the crucified and exalted Christ cannot be used to force the entire book of Revelation into a scheme of prophecy pertaining to the second advent and the events to take place at the second advent. Nor can it be employed to prove the contention of the modern "eschatological" school of interpretation. According to this school the Christian community of the first century was in such constant expectancy of the immediate return of the Lord that their whole outlook on life and the world was dominated by this expectancy. This view has in effect made of the Christian community of the first century an eschatological cult. According to this view the book of Revelation is a product of this expectancy, heightened by the persecution and crisis under Domitian.

There is something to be said on the other side of this question, however. The character of the Gospel of John in its relation to the eschatological question has not been given due consideration. Much is made by scholars of the idea that John "spiritualizes" the *Parousia*, or second coming, and that the Gospel is noneschatological in its outlook. But scholars have failed to relate this fact to the probability that the Gospel and the Apocalypse were written in the same period and that both are products of the Ephesian school. The Gospel is plainly noneschatological in emphasis. Since it originated in the province of Asia, are we wrong in insisting that the Apocalypse, while apocalyptic in style, does not teach the immediacy of the return of Jesus? Is it reasonable to think that there should exist within the bounds of an area so small as that which embraced the Asian churches, in the same period of time, two views so opposed as the non-eschatological, represented by the Gospel of John, and the view that the return of Christ was imminent? There is no question but that the Apocalypse preserves the early teaching concerning the certainty of the Lord's return. This is seen at this point (1:7) and perhaps at others (22:7,12,20). And it seems certain that the author held before his readers the possibility of the Lord's return in his own time; but this does not mean that he prophesied that the Lord would return in the immediate future or that he was sending forth a scheme of events to take place with the Lord's return. The point we are insisting upon is that the author has retained the wholesome eschatological hope of early Christianity and that it is a wholesome expectation, even though it is clothed in the symbolism of apocalyptic. A wholesome expectation concerning the return of Christ has belonged to the Christian tradition from the beginning. The teaching concerning the second advent is the core of Christian eschatology. It should be said with emphasis that Christianity without its eschatological teaching is not Christianity.

The Author's Commission to Write.—1:9–20

The author of Revelation thought of himself as a prophet, not only in the ordinary New Testament sense of one who was endowed with the gift of inspired utterance. In this sense the prophetic office is referred to in 1 Corinthians 12:28 f.; 14:29,37; Ephesians 4:11. The author of the Apocalypse believed that he was called to revive the Old Testament office of *writing* prophet. He sees himself as falling heir to the mantle of Isaiah, Ezekiel, and others of the great writing prophets of old. He describes his own experience as similar to that of Ezekiel's in the matter of eating the little book in chapter 10, and he hears himself identified with the prophets in 22:9. The prophets of old were men commissioned of God to prophesy. It was necessary for a true prophet to be conscious of his call; he must write or speak with a "thus saith

29

the Lord." Isaiah, Jeremiah, and Ezekiel experienced visions in which they were impressed with the call of the Lord. They describe these visions as basis for their authority to speak for God. The prophet of Revelation is no exception to this rule that the prophet of God must give an account of his call and set forth the basis of his claim to speak with authority as God's messenger. In this section he explains his credentials and describes the vision by which he was authorized to write.

As a true prophet John identifies himself with the people to whom he is called to minister. He is "I, John"—one who is well known to them. He is a brother and sharer with them "in the tribulation and kingdom and patience in Jesus." This is a significant joining of "kingdom" with "tribulation" and "patience." The kingdom which he shares with his people is real and present. The kingdom of which he speaks is the reign or sovereignty of God in which all believers in Christ share by reason of his kingship; the author does not refer to a future kingdom to be realized upon the Lord's return. In the midst of tribulation, such kingdom or sovereignty is an actuality; its existence is compatible with the tribulation of believers. Jesus had said, "In the world ye have tribulation: but be of good cheer; I have overcome the world" (John 16:33). Therefore, John of the Apocalypse can speak of the patience which he also shares with his readers.

John could speak as a prophet because he had suffered as a prophet. He states that he "was in the isle that is called Patmos, for the word of God and the testimony of Jesus." The clear meaning of his words is that he had suffered exile because of his fidelity to the Word of God and because he had been faithful in his witness concerning Jesus. He had refused to offer a sacrifice before a statue of the emperor and utter the words *Kyrios Kaisar* ("Lord Caesar"). The penalty he suffered for his loyalty to Christ was banishment to the little island of Patmos, where he was probably forced to labor in the salt mines.

Again, John can claim that his message is the message of a prophet because his commission came to him when he was "in the Spirit." The prophet was always one who through the operation of the Spirit could be lifted out of himself to experience ecstasy and visions. John's ecstatic experience of call came to him on the "Lord's day," by which is meant, no doubt, the first day of the week; the day which the early Christians adopted as their day of worship because it was the day of the week on which the Lord arose from the grave. Doubtless John was thinking of his fellow Christians meeting, as was their custom, on the Lord's Day; and perchance in imagination he was worshiping with them when the Spirit came upon him and revealed to him the great mission to which he was called. He was to write what he was to see in vision and send it to the seven churches: Ephesus, Smyrna, Pergamum, Thyatira, Sardis, Philadelphia, and Laodicea.

The authentication of his commission is given to John in a vision of Christ as the great Son of man. The background of the vision is to be found in the book of Daniel. The Christ who appears to John is prefigured in the heavenly beings of Daniel's visions. These are described in Daniel 7:9,13, and 10:5-6. Apparently the Christ seen by John has assumed the characteristics of Jehovah, or "the ancient of days," as he is described in Daniel 7:9. "His head and his hair were white as white wool, white as snow." The "ancient of days" is described by Daniel as having "the hair of his head like pure wool" (7:9). The Christ of the Apocalypse is seen "in the midst of the seven golden candlesticks." The explanation of the "seven golden candlesticks" in 1:20 is that they represent the seven churches. Thus the Christ of the Apocalypse walks among the churches. He holds in his right hand seven stars which are the "angels of the seven churches," as is explained in 1:20. Who are these angels of the churches? Are they the pastors or bishops of the churches? Perhaps. Each letter is addressed to the "angel" of that particular church. If by "angels" is meant the pastors of the churches, Christ is represented in this vision as holding the pastors in his right hand. The symbolism suggests Christ's authority over the pastors, his power to hold them and direct them as he wills.

31

The sharp, two-edged sword which proceeds out of the mouth of the Son of man in John's vision is the symbol of the Christ's weapon of conquest and victory. In another vision the Seer will see Christ with this sharp sword proceeding from his mouth (19:15). This symbolism indicates that Christ's weapon of conquest and victory is the Word of God; the sword is no actual sword—it proceeds from his mouth, the source of the Christ's Word. In 19:13 it is said, "His name is called The Word of God."

The effect of the vision upon John is not unlike the experience of Daniel when he saw a similar vision (10:15–19). Like Daniel, John fell to the ground "as one dead"; but as Daniel was admonished, he was admonished to "fear not." In the experience of John, however, the assurance comes from One who is infinitely more worthy to give it; he is "the first and the last, and the Living one"; who can declare, "I was dead, and behold, I am alive for evermore, and I have the keys of death and of Hades."

John receives his commission to write direct from the glorified and exalted Christ. "Write therefore," he is commanded, "the things which thou sawest, and the things which are, and the things which shall come to pass hereafter." We should not miss the significance of the specific mention of the matters to be contained in John's book. The contents are to embrace more than prophecies of coming events. The author is to write the things which he "saw." The things the prophet "saw" could certainly include visions of things in heaven and on earth and of events of the past, present, and future. "The things which are" certainly refers to present realities, whether heavenly or of earth. These two specifications as to the contents of Revelation should warn the interpreter of the book that it is no mere plan of events to transpire at the end of the age. "The things which are" may certainly embrace great spiritual realities that are timeless and great doctrines, such as the sovereignty of God, redemption, etc. One of the arresting features of the Apocalypse is its emphasis upon such matters. But these have often been overlooked by interpreters in their zeal to see in Revelation a schematic treatment of last things. "The things which shall come to pass hereafter" is a formula indicative that the prophet has been commissioned to give a revelation of future events. Certainly the Apocalypse contains a prophecy of "things which must shortly come to pass." Apparently it was given to the author not only to prophesy concerning things shortly to come to pass but concerning things belonging to the long future. In all this reference to the revelation of the future there is no claim of the author that he is commissioned to give an outline of history or a scheme of things to transpire at the second advent of Christ.

Thus by the commission of the exalted Christ to the prophet we are led to approach with soberness and humility the message of the great book.

Chapter IV

THE LETTERS TO THE
SEVEN CHURCHES

THE letters to the seven churches are the most familiar portion of the book of Revelation. The reason for this is obvious—they are the most understandable portion. This fact emphasizes their dissimilarity with the remainder of the book. If the letters were not in the book as it has come to us, there would be no reason to believe they had ever been a part of it. A person reading Revelation can pass from the first chapter to the fourth without being conscious of any break in the narrative. This suggests that the author composed the letters separately and inserted them into the remaining portion of his work, perhaps, after the main portion of the book was completed.

But this in no sense suggests any lack of importance in the letters. They are not only an integral part of Revelation, but they shed much light upon the author's purpose and the manner in which he approached the problem that confronted him of awakening the churches to the seriousness of the impending crisis. The letters are also very suggestive in the light they shed upon the church life of the late first century.

The writing of letters was practiced widely among the churches and church leaders of the first century. By this means the churches maintained an intimacy of contact probably underestimated in its value and importance by modern interpreters of the New Testament. The letters of Paul, produced in the white heat of intense missionary labors, are illustrations of the importance of letters in the life and development of the churches. The letters to the seven churches are in this letter-writing tradition developed to such a high degree of skill by Paul.

But the letters of the Apocalypse have a character of their own. Unlike the letters of Paul, they have no meaning apart from the larger work to which they belong. Not only is each letter an integral part of the Apocalypse, but it belongs also to the seven. Again, the seven must in a sense be conceived of as one letter addressed to all the churches. It is clear that all the letters are intended for each church and that each letter is intended for all the churches.

Let it be said with emphasis that the churches addressed were actual churches. The author is not undertaking in these letters to give a series of prophecies concerning coming periods of the church age. The presence of these letters in Revelation serve to relate the entire book to an actual historical situation. The author visualizes these churches in their needs and struggles as they face what appears to be a rising storm of persecution. He sees his message as answering the needs of the men and women of flesh and blood who compose the congregations of these churches. This undeniable relation of the contents of Revelation to an actual existing situation assures the relevancy of the book to our own condition as Christians in the twentieth century. Human nature remains fairly constant through the passing of centuries. The weaknesses and sins which beset the churches in the first century are not uncommon in our own time. Similarities can be seen in conditions external to the churches then and now. The spiritual needs of men are always the same. Thus we are strengthened, by the presence of the letters, in our conviction that the Revelation speaks to our own time.

But why only seven letters? There were other churches in the province of Asia.[1] Has our author deliberately neglected them? Sir W. M. Ramsay has dealt with these and other ques-

[1] The existence of at least three of them, Colossae, Hierapolis, and Troas, is known from the New Testament. Doubtless there were scores of others.

tions in his well-known *The Letters to the Seven Churches of Asia.*[2] Little can be said here that will add anything to what has been said by Ramsay by way of introduction to an interpretation of the letters, and anything that is said must of necessity reflect the influence of his suggestive and valuable work.

The seven churches are *representative* of all the churches in the province of Asia and perhaps of all the churches in the empire. And as we seek to apply the great spiritual truths of Revelation to our own time, it is not beside the mark to say that they are representatives of the churches today.

These seven churches were chosen, according to Ramsay's view, because each of them was the center of a group of churches. Another consideration may have influenced their choice, Ramsay believes, and this was that each city named was a communications center situated on a very important circular route which, beginning at Ephesus, passed through the most cultured and historically pre-eminent part of the province.[8] The cities are named in the order in which a messenger would pass through them, beginning at Ephesus. The assumption is that John sent his book by messenger from Patmos and that the messenger stopped first at Ephesus, which is closest to the island of John's banishment, and from Ephesus passed on to the other cities in order. Reference to a map of the Province of Asia will show that the cities are named in the order in which a messenger would pass through them, going north from Ephesus to Smyrna, continuing north to Pergamum, turning at this point southeast to Thyatira, from here continuing almost due south to Sardis, and from here going southeast to Philadelphia and Laodicea. To complete the circuit, the messenger would return due west to Ephesus. Ramsay suggests that the highly developed postal systems of the Roman Government and private business enterprises were patterns followed by the early churches in

²London: Hodder and Stoughton, 1904. See especially chapters I, II, III, IV, XIV, XV, and XVI.

³*Ibid.*, chapters XV and XVI.

the exchange of letters and communications, and that John had the benefit of some such system in the despatch of Revelation to the seven churches. If, as is probable, each of the churches named was the center of a group of churches, it is reasonable to suppose that it assumed responsibility for the delivery of a copy of the Apocalypse to the sister churches in its area. This doubtless demanded that each of the seven churches should retain a copy of its own and perhaps reproduce copies for its neighboring sister congregations.

The letters reveal much that is interesting about church life in the late first century. One of the most arresting facts they reveal is the absence of a developed ecclesiasticism in church organization. This is quite significant when we give due consideration to the fact that the period in which we find ourselves is sixty-five years removed from Pentecost and the primitive church. There is no conception of the churches as "the church." The individuality of each church is recognized and respected; each is addressed separately. In no instance do we meet with the expression, "the church of Jesus Christ." At the same time each church is recognized as belonging to the wider circle of all the churches. Thus there is a remarkable blending of the independence of each church with the interdependence of all the churches. "He that hath an ear, let him hear what the Spirit saith to the churches," is an admonition that is addressed to each individual church. No bishop or overlord makes his appearance in these letters. The nearest approach to a "bishop" is the "angel" who is addressed, if indeed it can be said that the "angel" is the "bishop" or pastor. It is conceivable that the "angel" represents the church in the sum total of its spiritual existence; but however this may be, the "angel" is no overlord who may control the life of the church. The exalted Christ is represented in each instance as addressing the "angel" of the church. But it is plain that Christ speaks directly to each church and its members; he is the real head of each congregation; he and he alone is endowed with authority to warn, to commend, to promise reward.

Thus we observe that even so late as A.D. 95 the ecclesiasticism and episcopacy which engulfed the churches in the second and third centuries had not emerged when the Apocalypse was written. In the letters to the seven churches are revealed the simplicity and democracy of church organization which characterized the church life of the entire New Testament period. The letters to the seven churches confirm our faith in the belief that the simple, democratic form of church organization and government was the form created by Christ himself and that form which is most in keeping with his design and spirit.

Yet other characteristics of the church life of this period which strike the reader rather forcefully are the frailty and human weakness so evident in the membership of the churches. Only two of the churches, Smyrna and Philadelphia, escape condemnation because of the presence of sin within the church. Ephesus, Pergamum, Sardis, and Laodicea are bluntly warned to "repent," while a similar warning is given to a group within the church at Thyatira. Apparently the most serious malady afflicting these churches was the presence and work within them of a heretical sect called the Nicolaitans, or Balaamites. The probability is that "the woman called Jezebel," who was active in the church at Thyatira, was a leader in this sect. This being true, these Nicolaitans, or Balaamites, were active in two of the churches, Pergamum and Thyatira. Perhaps all the churches were in some peril from the activities of this sect. We learn that they had made, without success, an attempt to invade the church at Ephesus. It can be inferred from the heat with which John speaks of the teaching and work of this sect that the churches were in rather grave peril as a result of the activity of these heretics. John viewed their strength with alarm, and recognized that the churches must rid themselves of their evil influence if they were to be able to stand firmly in their resistance to emperor worship and its attendant evils.

But there were other sins in the churches to be dealt with. Ephesus had left her "first love"; Sardis had a "name to live"

38

but was "dead"; Laodicea was "neither cold nor hot." All this is but another evidence of the fact that from the beginning the churches could never claim perfection. The primitive church in Jerusalem was cursed with bickering and with the presence of the liars, Ananias and Sapphira. Paul found it necessary to deal often with moral problems in the churches established by him. Churches have been good, bad, and indifferent through the centuries, but no single one of them has ever been able to achieve moral perfection. But the church of Jesus Christ has survived, and will survive, despite the moral imperfection of the churches. In this review of the life of the churches of the Apocalypse, we are confronted with the sad fact that unregenerate individuals can hold membership in a church; but, on the other hand, we are impressed with the grave concern this fact gives to the Seer of Patmos as he visualizes the churches in mortal combat with the imperial Roman power. This concern reminds us that the presence of evil within the churches is never a matter to be taken lightly despite the fact that the churches never were and never can be morally perfect.

The attention we have given to the evil in these churches should not blind us to the fact that there was much that was good in them also. John did not overlook the element of strength that could be seen in them. He recognized the "toil and patience" of Ephesus and the fact that this church could not "bear evil men." He rejoiced in the fact that Smyrna, though poverty stricken in worldly goods, was rich in the things of the Spirit. He was happy to represent the Son of God as saying to the church at Thyatira, "I know thy works, and thy love and faith and ministry and patience, and that thy last works are more than the first." Even to Sardis he could represent Christ as saying, "Thou hast a few names in Sardis that did not defile their garments." Of all the churches, none brought more joy by its faithfulness than Philadelphia. Christ had set before this church a door "which none can shut," because she had kept his word and not denied his name. And John realizes that even lukewarm

Laodicea can yet claim the love of Christ, for he says to this church, "As many as I love, I reprove and chasten."

The author follows a fairly uniform pattern in the composition of the letters. This can be illustrated as follows:

(1) The salutation: (a) to the "angel" of the church, the "angel" representing either the pastor or the composite spiritual existence of the congregation; (b) from Jesus Christ revealed in seven characteristics of his glorified being.
(2) A commendation for good works and faithfulness. Absent only in the case of Laodicea.
(3) An accusation concerning sin. Present in all the letters except those to Smyrna and Philadelphia.
(4) An exhortation. Present in all.
(5) A warning. In all the letters except those to Smyrna and Philadelphia.
(6) A promised reward. In all the letters.
(7) The sevenfold refrain: "He that hath an ear, let him hear what the Spirit saith to the churches." Found in all the letters.

Ephesus: the church that left its first love.—2:1–7

Ephesus was one of the most important and interesting cities in the empire. It was the capital of the province of Asia and was important as a center of business and trade. It was the western terminus of a great system of roads. It was a free city, its governing bodies consisting of a board of magistrates, a senate, and a popular assembly. It was celebrated in the ancient world as the center of the worship of Artemis or Diana and as the seat of the great temple of this goddess, regarded as one of the seven wonders of the world in the first century. The East met the West at Ephesus. Here were to be found in great numbers the cults and mysteries of the East, as well as the philosophies of Greece and the West. Ephesus bulked large in the history of Christianity. Paul made the city

40

his headquarters for some three years, and, according to tradition, the apostle John made his home here in his latter days. It was perhaps the strongest center of Christianity in the last years of the first century.

The church at Ephesus was doubtless regarded as the leading church of the province. It was founded by the apostle Paul at the beginning of his ministry at Ephesus in A.D. 52. Thus the church had been in existence a little more than forty years. Ephesus had been well-grounded from the beginning in the meaning of Christian love. The apostle Paul wrote his first letter to the Corinthians from Ephesus. It is reasonable to believe that the great teaching on love in the thirteenth chapter of that epistle was rehearsed many times in the hearing of the Ephesian brethren. After Paul's passing, the great Apostle of Love, John, came to Ephesus, and he doubtless left a deep impression in the minds of the believers there concerning the greatness of Christian love. In the light of these facts, we can better understand the poignant accusation in the letter to Ephesus: "I have this against thee, that thou didst leave thy first love."

The "first love" of Ephesus was the love that her people knew and practiced in earlier days, the love that had been handed down as a tradition from the great apostle Paul and confirmed by John the beloved. Of all the churches, Ephesus was equipped to appreciate and practice *agapē*, Christian love; and yet with the passing of the years she had lost that ardor with which she once demonstrated her love for God and man. This was the one sin that calls forth from the glorified Christ, speaking through his messenger from Patmos, an expression of heartfelt disappointment. In this declension from her "first love," Ephesus is a type of that church which permits the growth of formalism and increasing interest in worldly things to reduce the warmth of brotherhood and the practice of unselfishness toward others.

But Ephesus was strong in her resistance to evil men who, posing as Christian leaders, sought to teach false doctrine within the church. "I know thy works," Ephesus is told, "and thy toil and patience, and that thou canst not bear evil men, and didst try them that call themselves apostles, and they are not, and didst find them false; and thou hast patience and didst bear for my name's sake, and hast not grown weary." Again the resistance of the church to evil men is emphasized: "But this thou hast, that thou hatest the works of the Nicolaitans, which I also hate." The steadfast resistance of the Ephesian church to the heretical Nicolaitans is evidence of the fact that it was at this time still a strong and spiritually alive church. The churches at Pergamum and Thyatira had failed to deal with these heretics as Ephesus had done; their presence in these churches threatened their very existence. The success of the heretics in these two churches suggests their strength in the province of Asia. It is at this point that we should attempt to identify these disturbers and disrupters of church life in the last decade of the first century.

It seems clear that the Nicolaitans, the Balaamites of 2:14, and the followers of the woman Jezebel, mentioned in 2:20, are all of the same sect. After the description of the Balaamites in 2:14, there follows this statement: "So hast thou also some that hold the teaching of the Nicolaitans in like manner." Even though the Balaamites and the Nicolaitans could be regarded as separate groups, this statement is to be interpreted as meaning that both groups held to the same beliefs. According to the description given of the Balaamites in the letter to the church at Pergamum, these heretics were like Balaam who "taught Balak to cast a stumblingblock before the children of Israel, to eat things sacrificed to idols, and to commit fornication" (2:14). In the letter to Thyatira the woman Jezebel is indicted in these words: "She teacheth and seduceth my servants to commit fornication, and to eat things sacrificed to idols" (2:20). It is clear that the chief evils resulting from the teaching of these heretics were fornication and the eating of things sacrificed to idols.

Further light on the character of this heretical sect which plagued the Asian churches may be gained by reference to the Old Testament characters used in connection with

42

descriptions of the sect. These characters are Balaam, Balak, and Jezebel. Balak was the heathen king of Moab who attempted to compel his prophet Balaam to curse the children of Israel without success (Numbers 23–24).

Jezebel was the queen who acted as patroness of the pagan prophets of Baal and Ashtoreth (1 Kings 18:19). (Ashtoreth was the principal female divinity of the Phenicians, and Baal was the chief male divinity). It will be recalled that Jezebel was the archenemy of Jehovah's prophet, Elijah, and sought to kill him after the slaying of the prophets of Baal at the brook Kishon. Apparently Balaam and Jezebel appear in the author's account because he may use them as notorious examples of persons who caused God's people to sin. The complaint against Balaam is that he "taught Balak to cast a stumblingblock before the children of Israel" (2:14). The ancient Jezebel is the prototype of the Jezebel of the church at Thyatira because it may be said of the latter, "she teacheth my servants to commit fornication, and to eat things sacrificed to idols" (2:20). In her sponsorship of the prophets and religion of Ashtoreth and Baal, Jezebel, wife of Ahab, king of Israel, encouraged the worship of these heathen divinities by the Israelites and the practice by them of the licentious rites connected with the worship of Baal and Ashtoreth. One of the evils connected with this religion was the practice of sexual orgies.

The use of the pagan prophet Balaam in this connection may not be altogether clear, for we recall that while the king Balak desired the prophet to curse Israel, Balaam was able only to bless Jehovah's people. However, immediately after the recording of this incident it is related that "the people began to play the harlot with the daughters of Moab: for they called the people unto the sacrifice of their gods: and the people did eat, and bowed down to their gods. And Israel joined himself unto Baal-peor: and the anger of Jehovah was kindled against Israel" (Numbers 25:1–3). After the destruction of the Midianites, Moses said to his officers concerning the captured Moabite women: "Behold, these caused the children of Israel, through the counsel of Balaam, to commit trespass against Jehovah in the matter of Peor, and so the plague was among the congregation of Jehovah" (Numbers 31:16).

This study of the Old Testament typology used in the description of the Nicolaitans points to the conclusion that they were guilty of some form of idolatry. They are accused outright of fornication and eating things sacrificed to idols. The eating of things sacrificed to idols in earlier days had been an offense to Jewish members of the church. The practice was prohibited by the decree of the Council of Jerusalem. (See Acts 15:29.) Paul discouraged the practice, but he set no great store by its importance. (See 1 Corinthians 8.) Paul's attitude shows that the eating of meat that had been sacrificed to idols and later sold in the markets did not involve worship of the idol by the believer who purchased the meat. At the time Revelation was written, Jewish influence in the church had greatly waned. It is probable therefore that the eating of things sacrificed to idols meant something more in the Province of Asia in A.D. 95 than it did in A.D. 49 when the decree of the Jerusalem Council was written and in A.D. 55 when the First Epistle to the Corinthians was written. It involved at the later date, no doubt, some connection with emperor worship. The Nicolaitans were probably a sect within Christianity which had come to terms with the officials of the emperor cult and who demonstrated their loyalty to the emperor by making a sacrifice before the statue of the emperor. To this practice the author of the Apocalypse applies the old formula, "eating things sacrificed to idols." Such a description was used for protective reasons to conceal a direct reference to the emperor and at the same time to emphasize the heinousness of the practice.

The term "fornication" is probably to be understood here in its natural sense and not as symbolical of the infidelity of the Nicolaitans in worshiping the Caesar. The sect was doubtless guilty of teaching a form of Christianity which encouraged sexual irregularities and loose morals. This teaching

44

probably derived from one of the forms of Gnosticism which plagued the church in the late first century and in the second century. This school of Gnostics taught that it was impossible for the soul to be contaminated by sin. Such belief encouraged immorality, and since it gave encouragement to evil practices under a cloak of religion, it suggested similarity with the evil rites connected with the worship of the old heathen deities, Baal and Ashtoreth. A sect holding such views with respect to religion and morals would find no difficulty in effecting a compromise with Caesar worship. Having gone so far as to make a complete separation between religion and morals, there could be no point in insisting that the worship of the image of Caesar was a form of infidelity. But the Ephesian church saw it otherwise. Its membership recognized that the Nicolaitans were dangerous heretics who violated the fundamental principles of Christianity. They saw that their nefarious doctrines and practices were perversions of the great truths handed down to them by the apostles. They hated the works of the Nicolaitans and for this hatred received, through the Seer of Patmos, the praise of the exalted Christ.

The type of Gnosticism represented by these Nicolaitans has reappeared from time to time in the life of Christianity. The ancient Gnostics, by their doctrine that Christ only appeared to be a man, removed him from the realm of history and reality and opened the way for disparagement of his earthly life and ethical teaching. The result was a cleavage between religion and morals. Religion became a matter of doctrine and mystical beliefs and practices. He who believed and met the demands of a system of rites was saved; for him the indulgence of the body was a matter of indifference. It is not unusual in our own time to meet with beliefs and practices of this sort. There is a modern Gnosticism of this sort with which churches have to contend. It can be recognized and designated as the old heresy come to life. For it the churches should have no more tolerance than the church at Ephesus had when she hated the works of the Nicolaitans.

Smyrna: the rich poor church.—2:8-11

Ramsay called Smyrna "the city of life" because it had survived destruction and was rebuilt on two occasions. The city
strove with Ephesus and Pergamum for the honor of being the
"first of Asia." The city was the seat of a strong Jewish community. When Polycarp, the bishop of Smyrna, was martyred
in A.D. 155, the Jews joined with the pagans in accusing him
of hostility to the state religion. They united with his accusers
in demanding his death and helped to gather fagots and sticks
to light the fire in which he was burned to death. Apparently
there was deep hostility between the congregation of the
church at Smyrna and the Jewish community when the Apocalypse was written. The Christ who speaks to the church is
represented as saying, "I know thy tribulation, and thy poverty (but thou art rich), and the blasphemy of them that say
they are Jews, and they are not, but are a synagogue of
Satan."

These are strong words. They show how wide the breach
had grown between the Christian community and the Jews.
Paul and the early missionaries began their work in the synagogues. The Gentile "God-fearers" of the synagogues had
often formed nuclei of early Christian congregations. In the
earliest days Jewish Christians attended synagogue and
church. But here at Smyrna the break which the apostle Paul
strove to avert has become complete. The Jews are not conceived of as true Jews at all. The implication of the charge is
that only Christian Jews are the true Jews. The position is not
out of keeping with the position of the apostle Paul, who
maintained that Christianity was the fulfilment of Judaism.
The synagogue of the Jews is referred to in this letter to the
church at Smyrna as "a synagogue of Satan." The language
seems harsh and must reflect some rather violent opposition
to the Christian church by the Jews at Smyrna. The opposition was a part of the "tribulation" which the church had
borne.

But the outstanding distinction of the church at Smyrna

46

was the fact that the congregation, though poor in material goods, was rich in spiritual things. "Thou art rich," the Smyrneans are told. Doubtless the overshadowing wealth of the Jewish community had given to the poverty-stricken Christians a sense of inferiority. They are reminded that true wealth does not consist in material affluence. Had not Jesus taught the perils of wealth and encouraged his followers to renounce earthly possessions in exchange for eternal life? Perhaps the church at Smyrna had forgotten this and needed to be reminded of the riches of the life in Christ.

The church at Smyrna is faced with yet more tribulation. Imprisonment awaits some of her members. "Ye shall have tribulation ten days," the church is warned. "Ten days" is one of the enigmatical numbers used by the author to indicate a brief period of time. The expression is not to be taken as denoting a literal period of ten days. The impending tribulation is doubtless a part of the general persecution the author foresees as rising against the church. Smyrna will need to remember the true riches when the persecution comes home to her. The church is exhorted to be faithful even unto death. The promised reward for fidelity is "the crown of life" to be bestowed by the Christ himself. The crown promised to the faithful is the crown which belongs to eternal life; it is the symbol of that reward which is granted to all the faithful at the end of their earthly life, a reward which is consonant with faithful stewardship in the kingdom of·God.

Pergamum: the church that was close to Satan's throne.—2:12-17

The earliest city of Pergamum was built on a hill one thousand feet high. This hill became the site of the acropolis and chief buildings of the later city. Pergamum was famed for its structures in honor of Zeus and other gods. On the great hill towering above the city stood the temple and many altars to heathen deities. As early as 29 B.C. a temple was dedicated at Pergamum to the Emperor Augustus and Rome

47

by the provincial synod. The city thus won recognition early for its allegiance to the emperor cult.

The church at Pergamum dwelt under the shadow of the altar to the emperor. It is set down to her credit that she did not deny the name of Christ, even when one of her members was slain because of his faithfulness. This man Antipas was perhaps one of the first of the martyrs to die in the persecution of the church because of its refusal to compromise with emperor worship. Pergamum deserves the more praise because the church has remained faithful in the shadow of the altar to the emperor, which is described as "Satan's throne." But, in spite of her record of loyalty, Pergamum faces grave danger. The peril that now confronts her is from within the church itself. So long as the enemies of Christ could be clearly identified by their position outside the church, there was little to fear. Antipas had given his life rather than bow before the emperor's altar. All could see that the officials of the emperor cult were priests of Satan; but now there had appeared within the church a group who called themselves Christians but who were quite willing to make their peace with the Roman authorities. They were the Nicolaitans, who are described as holding "the teaching of Balaam, who taught Balak to cast a stumblingblock before the children of Israel, to eat things sacrificed to idols, and to commit fornication."

Thus the church at Pergamum faced the serious peril of disintegration from the effects of heresy within. Ephesus had been more successful, as we have seen, in resisting the assaults of the Nicolaitans, but the heretics had gained a foothold in the congregation at Pergamum. The church as a whole is held responsible for the presence of the Nicolaitans. It is warned, "Repent, therefore; or else I come to thee quickly, and I will make war against them with the sword of my mouth." The urgent admonition "repent" is a challenge to the church to purge itself of these heretics. The warfare to be waged against them by Christ himself, "with the sword of my mouth," is the warfare which is shaping up against the Roman imperial power and its satellites. This is indicated by the fact that Christ appears here in the character of the warrior who is described in 19:11–16 as coming forth to make war with the beast and his allies: "And out of his mouth proceedeth a sharp sword, that with it he should smite the nations" (19:15). The Nicolaitans, by this identification of the Christ who will make war against them with the Christ who will lead in the great battle against the beast and his allies, are placed in the camp of the enemies of Christ. They are the objects of the thrust of the same weapon, the sword that proceeds from the mouth of the conquering Christ. This is the sword of the *word* of Christ. This word is a word of appeal to those who will hear, but it is a word of terrible judgment upon the enemies of God. It is this pronouncement of the word of judgment to be made by Christ against the enemies of God which awaits the Nicolaitan heretics of Pergamum. The crisis in which the Pergamum congregation stands is in this: that unless it repents of the presence of these heretics, it must stand in the awkward position of facing the wrath of the conquering Christ as he goes forth to battle against the imperial Roman power, for within the Pergamum church are those who, though professing the name of Christ, are allies of the enemies of Christ.

Pergamum is promised a reward for faithfulness. "To him that overcometh, to him will I give of the hidden manna, and I will give him a white stone, and upon the stone a new name written, which no one knoweth but he that receiveth it." Manna was sustenance and life to the Israelites in the wilderness. Here it is the symbol of the life-giving spiritual food which will be given to those who remain faithful to Christ. The white stone inscribed with a "new name" is to be understood as in contrast with the charms worn by the worshipers of heathen gods and inscribed with the names of the deities. Such charms were supposed to protect the wearers from harm. The "white stone" promised to the faithful believer at Pergamum would be inscribed with the name of Christ. The "white stone" is a symbol of the protection guaranteed to every believer by his unwavering loyalty to Christ.

49

Thyatira: the church that harbored a Jezebel.—2:18-29

Thyatira, situated forty miles southeast of Pergamum, was a small city in the first century and was the least important of all the cities of the seven churches. But it was a center of some commercial activity, for there were a number of trade guilds located here. Lydia, the good woman who provided a home for Paul and Silas and the first Christian congregation at Philippi, was a native of Thyatira.

Doubtless the church at Thyatira was small, but it had a good record of faithfulness. No church of the seven receives praise for more evidences of good works than Thyatira. In the letter addressed to the church there are these words of commendation: "I know thy works, and thy love and faith and ministry and patience, and that thy last works are more than the first." Here is an impressive list of virtues certainly: (1) works; (2) love; (3) faith; (4) ministry—that is, service; (5) patience—or, better, steadfastness (Greek, *hupomonē*). In greater testimony of Thyatira's loyalty to the cause of Christ is her growth in good works. The church is commended because her "last works are more than the first." And so we have before us the picture of a church that has remained faithful through the years and has by the increase of its good works proved its spiritual vitality and growth in Christian experience.

The one fault of the church at Thyatira was that the congregation tolerated an evil woman as one of its leaders. This woman is called Jezebel. The name of Ahab's heathen queen was given to her, as we have seen in the discussion of the Nicolaitans and the church at Ephesus, because of the similarity of her conduct to that of her Old Testament prototype. The ancient Jezebel was patroness of the prophets of Baal and Ashtoreth. She was the personification of wickedness in that she led the Israelites into idolatry and the practice of the immoralities connected with the worship of the heathen deities. The Jezebel of Thyatira was undoubtedly a member of the Nicolaitan sect. We have seen that these here-

50

tics doubtless belonged to the school of Gnostics which encouraged immoral conduct under the cloak of religion. Additional light on the belief and practices of the sect is found in this letter. Christ addresses himself to the church at one point in these words: "But to you, I say, to the rest that are in Thyatira, as many as have not this teaching, who know not the deep things of Satan, as they are wont to say; I cast upon you none other burden." From this statement it may be inferred that the Nicolaitans were those who claimed to know "the deep things of Satan" and taunted the Christians who did not follow their teaching with the charge that they (the orthodox Christians) did not know "the deep things of Satan." One of the beliefs of the branch of Gnosticism represented in the Nicolaitans was that deeds done in the body could not hurt the soul. The effect of such teaching was to encourage the believer that he was "above" sin; he could not sin, it mattered not what his conduct might be. People who took such a view of religion and morals might easily claim to know "the deep things of Satan." That is to say, they believed that they were well acquainted with the mind and the method of Satan—so well acquainted with them, in fact, that they could outwit Satan and follow the pleasures of the flesh without sinning. Apparently the belief of those Gnostics was that by esoteric initiation into the mysteries of the other world they had gained knowledge which enabled them to outwit Satan.

The appeal of this type of thinking to unstable and poorly indoctrinated Christians must have been quite strong. A system which afforded at the same time both the assurance of salvation and freedom to indulge in the pleasures of the flesh would make headway among superficial believers. An added appeal of such a system was its emphasis upon mysticism and knowledge. The so-called knowledge or *gnosis* which only the truly initiated could possess came by means of mystical apprehension of spiritual realities. This, and all other forms of Gnosticism, was most heretical in its teaching concerning the person of Christ. The docetic Gnostics, to which these Nicolaitans must have belonged, held that Christ in his earthly

51

life only appeared to be a man. This was an assault upon the incarnation, the central doctrine of the Christian religion. By this violent removal of Christ from history and the actualities of human experience, the heretical docetic Gnostics were able to make easy disposition of the ethical imperatives of Christianity. Since these belonged to the earthly life and ministry of Jesus, they were of no great importance. It was by such violent handling of truth that the Gnostics gave rise to sects like the Nicolaitans, who, by calmly making a separation between religion and morals, encouraged immoral indulgences under the cover of religion.

The Jezebel at Thyatira was a woman of prominence and influence. Some of the texts read "thy woman Jezebel," which, correctly rendered, would be "thy *wife* Jezebel." It has been suggested that she was the wife of the pastor of the church, on the assumption that the "angel," to whom the letter is addressed, is the pastor. It is not necessary to draw this conclusion, however. If this is the correct reading—and it is quite probable that it is—the woman is pictured as the "wife" of the church in order that the parallel with the case of the Old Testament Jezebel may be more apparent. By the use of the expression "thy wife," the author suggests that the same sort of unholy alliance exists between the church at Thyatira and this evil woman as that which existed between Ahab, king of Israel, and his heathen wife. By such an unholy alliance God's people had been led into gross sin in days past. The suggestion of the Old Testament typology is that God's people at Thyatira will be corrupted in the same manner.

The woman had been given opportunity to repent but had refused. She persisted in her sin and continued to lead Christians astray. A warning of certain punishment is given for those who continue to follow her. They will be cast into a bed with her, where they will suffer great tribulation. The bed of sordid pleasure will become one of pain and anguish. Her children (her followers) will be killed. All this is a warning of the inevitable judgment to be visited upon these enemies of Christ who masquerade as his followers.

The faithful at Thyatira are urged to "hold fast till I come." The letter represents Christ as speaking. His words are a reminder to the church of the ever-present possibility of the Lord's return. The reward for faithfulness is a share in the authority of the victorious Christ. "And he that overcometh, and he that keepeth my works to the end, to him will I give authority over the nations: and he shall rule them with a rod of iron, as the vessels of the potter are broken to shivers; as I also have received of my Father: and I will give him the morning star." The "rod of iron" was the strong stick, tipped with iron, used by the shepherd to guard his flock. It is a symbol here of the Messiah's rule. The faithful followers of Christ will participate in that rule. The faithful believer will share in that which the Father has apportioned to the Son —"I will give him the morning star." The morning star, brightest of the heavens, is a symbol of the greatness and glory of the Christ in which all those who love him to the end will share.

Sardis: the church that had a name to live but was dead.—3:1-6

"The City of Death" is the appellation given to Sardis by Ramsay. He sees a reflection of the character of the city in the condition of the church. The city, although built upon what appeared to be an impregnable mountain 1,500 feet high, had suffered two disastrous invasions, the first by Cyrus, the second three hundred and twenty years later by Antiochus the Great. The city suffered a disastrous earthquake in A.D. 17. As a result of the calamity the Emperor Tiberius remitted its taxes for five years and made a contribution to the city equal to approximately $1,700,000. The city had declined in power and influence so that at the time Revelation was written it was one of the lesser cities of the province. The patron goddess of the city was Cybele.

No church save Laodicea, of all the seven, had declined so far in its spiritual life as had the church at Sardis, if the melancholy indictment the letter contains is to be taken as a reflection of its true condition. Truly the sad state of the church parallels the lifeless condition of the city. Almost we may apply to Sardis the appellation, "The Church of Death." "Thou hast a name that thou livest, and thou art dead. . . . I have found no works of thine perfected before my God." What was the malady that had brought Sardis so low? No mention is made of the work of Nicolaitans here. This is not evidence that the heretics had not been active in this congregation. It is possible that, like locusts, they had done their devastating work and had passed on. Of this we cannot be certain. It seems, however, that outwardly the church gave the appearance of life. It had a name to live. It continued in its organizational life and functions. It was still recognized as a church. Its building, its form, its worship, its ritual—these all testified to the fact that, as a body calling itself a church, Sardis still existed. But it was like the carcass of a man who appeared to be living—the breath of life, the vital spark, had disappeared. And so Sardis stood an empty shell of its former self—an organization but not a living organism.

"I have found no works of thine perfected before my God." These mournful words reveal the sickness that led to the death of Sardis. Here was a church that maintained its organization and carried through with its worship and ritual but failed to practice the true religion it had been taught. The expression of a vital experience with Christ had been neglected. The church received but did not give, and, like the Dead Sea, became a reservoir of death. It failed to understand that Christian experience remains vital through the expression in deed of that which is professed in words. It neglected the love and brotherhood a church must practice to remain a true church of Christ; it failed to evangelize and win sinners to Christ; it did not keep alive the fires of missionary zeal and stewardship of possessions so essential to the growth of a church of Jesus Christ.

And yet there is hope even where death reigns. There are

some "things" in the church at Sardis that may be revived. "Establish the things that remain, which were ready to die" —this is the exhortation that comes to a church which to all appearances is dead. The expression of this hope is possible because of the presence in the church of the sparks of certain Christian virtues. Perhaps these "things" refer to the church's organization and worship, and perchance its creed. If these are the sparks of the dying embers of a once more vigorous life, they can be fanned into a flame. To add greater hope to the prospect of revival is the presence of a small group in the church who have not been caught by the creeping death. "But thou hast a few names in Sardis that did not defile their garments." This little group of the faithful is a foundation upon which reconstruction can begin. The affirmation of their fidelity suggests that the Nicolaitans may have had much to do with the condition of the church at Sardis after all. These few faithful ones "did not defile their garments." The malady which had stricken the church was one which brought moral defilement with it. It is highly suggestive of the Nicolaitan heresy in its damaging work at Pergamum and Thyatira. If the suggestion be a safe guide, then Sardis stands as a ghostly monument to the spreading death of Gnosticism among the churches in the last decade of the first century. The church that had a name to live but was dead stands, in this case, as a mute testimony of the inevitable doom of all churches in which the earthly life of Jesus is disparaged and division is made between religion and morals.

But even a Sardis may repent. And so the church that was dead is called by Christ to live. "Remember therefore how thou hast received and didst hear; and keep it and repent." Sardis in her repenting must give in keeping with what she has received; she must speak and act in keeping with that which she has heard. Thus is repentance rightly interpreted as a change of mind which issues in action consonant with the change. Such repentance is Sardis' hope of rising from the dead. The penalty of failure to repent could be the sudden appearance of Christ in judgment. "If therefore thou shalt not watch, I will come as a thief, and thou shalt not know what hour I will come upon thee." In effect the church is told, "Live in expectation of the Lord's judgment and you will live right."

The faithful at Sardis are encouraged by the promise of a threefold reward that will be bestowed upon every loyal believer: (1) he will be "arrayed in white garments"; (2) his name will not be blotted out of the book of life; (3) his name will be confessed by Christ before the Father in heaven and his angels. The white garments are symbols of the moral purity and the heavenly righteousness which will be the possession of all true believers at the judgment. The "white garments" of the faithful provide a sharp contrast with the "defiled" garments of the members of the church who had fallen victim of the malady that had brought death to the church. The security of the faithful Christian is emphasized by the promise that his name will not be blotted out of the book of life. The honor he will receive is seen in the assurance that his name will be confessed by Christ before the Father and his angels.

Philadelphia: the church with a door of opportunity set before it.—3:7–13

If Smyrna was the "rich poor church," Philadelphia was the "strong weak church." An opened door of opportunity stood before this church because, even though it had "little power," it had kept the Word of Christ and had not denied his name. With Smyrna it shared the honor of greater fidelity to the gospel than the others of the seven. It would appear that the writer of the letters to the churches intended to mark Philadelphia as the choicest of all the seven. The testimony of the exalted Christ speaking through his interpreter places Philadelphia upon a pedestal of honor which she has occupied through the centuries. The characteristics of this church have made of her a model for all others to follow.

In his *Letters to the Seven Churches*, Ramsay recognizes

interesting parallels in the character of the church and of the city in which it was situated. He calls Philadelphia "the missionary city" because it was founded to promote Graeco-Asiatic civilization and to spread the Greek language and manners in the eastern parts of Lydia and Phrygia. The missionary character of the church is seen in the fact that there had been set before the church "a door opened." This door had been opened by none other than the Christ himself. He is described as "he that hath the key of David, he that openeth and none shall shut, and that shutteth and none openeth." The reference is to Isaiah 22:22, which contains a prophecy concerning Eliakim, the son of Hilkiah. The prophecy was that Eliakim would receive "the key of the house of David." This would make him the steward of the house of Hezekiah, the king, with the authority to exercise the power of a steward. The steward of Hezekiah's court is a type of Christ here. The Messiah, who is the son of David, holds the keys of the messianic kingdom. It is his authority to open these doors. He has opened a door of the kingdom in front of the church at Philadelphia. It is a door of opportunity such as Paul saw opened before him at Ephesus (1 Corinthians 16:9) and at Troas (2 Corinthians 2:12). It was a door of great missionary opportunity. The door had been opened because Philadelphia had been faithful to the gospel and to past opportunities. There was happy assurance for the church in the fact that the door had been opened by Christ and that no one had the power to close it.

Ramsay draws another parallel between the church and the city. The city was in a region visited often by earthquakes. In A.D. 17 a great earthquake destroyed twelve cities of the Lydian Valley, including Sardis and Philadelphia. When the great earthquake came, many of the inhabitants went outside the city to dwell, while those who remained in the city in patched-up houses lived in constant dread of a recurrence of the shocks. When the historian Strabo wrote in A.D. 20, many of the inhabitants were living outside the city in huts for fear of recurring shocks. In the light of these facts, two of

57

the promises made to the church may be the better appreciated. One of these was, "I also will keep thee from the hour of trial"; the other, "He that overcometh, I will make him a pillar in the temple of my God, and he shall go out thence no more." To people who had known the dread of fleeing a city being destroyed by an earthquake and who had awaited in terror the recurrence of shocks, these promises of security would be most welcome. "The hour of trial" apparently refers to the persecution in prospect for this church and others as a result of the enforcement of the policy of the emperor requiring that he be paid divine honors. Evidently this persecution had not yet reached Philadelphia. "I also will keep thee from the hour of trial" cannot be interpreted, in the light of other passages in Revelation, as a promise that the Philadelphian Christians will escape the persecution. When John has the vision of the souls of the martyrs underneath the altar and hears their questioning cry, "How long," he hears the reply, "that they should rest yet for a little time, until their fellow-servants also and their brethren, who should be killed even as they were, should have fulfilled *their course*" (6:9-11).

There is no promise in the book of Revelation that God's people shall escape suffering and death, but there is the promise that no harm can come to their souls. This is the burden of chapter 7, which contains the vision of the sealing of the servants of God. The promise contained in the letter to the church at Philadelphia seems to be of a similar nature. The warning, "I come quickly," follows immediately and raises the question as to whether the reference here is not to the final tribulation connected with the second advent. The expression, "I come quickly," cannot be definitely applied to the second advent; it may as well be interpreted as a warning of the pending judgment of Christ in the immediate situation confronting the churches. Pergamum was warned, "Repent therefore; or else I come to thee quickly, and I will make war against them with the sword of my mouth" (2:16). The implication here is that if the church repents and purges itself of the heretical Nicolaitans, Christ will not come quickly to make war against them with the sword of his mouth. But even if the expression is to be referred to the second advent, it is not necessary to believe that by the use of the adverb "quickly" the author intends to fix the coming of the Lord as immediate, for "quickly" may also mean "suddenly" or "unexpectedly." "The hour of trial" was to come upon the "whole inhabited earth," for this is the meaning of the Greek word *oikoumenē*. It was to "try" or "tempt" them that dwell upon the earth. Apparently this "trial" or "tempting" is to affect all dwellers upon the earth, whereas the whole tenor of the New Testament doctrine of last things suggests the escape of God's people from the sufferings of the final tribulation.

We conclude that the promise to the church at Philadelphia is one of help and succor for the impending persecution faced by all the churches. Incidentally, the opened door of missionary opportunity for Philadelphia would have very little meaning if the end of the age was just at hand.

The promise, "He that overcometh, I will make him a pillar in the temple of my God, and he shall go out thence no more," is the better understood, according to Ramsay, in the light of the experience of the people of Philadelphia with earthquakes. A pillar is a stable thing. A pillar supporting the temple of God is a happy figure of stability to hold before the earthquake-conscious Philadelphians. The promise, "He shall go out thence no more," would have vivid meaning for people who had been forced to leave their tottering homes to live outside the city. The promise here is of spiritual security in the midst of temporal insecurity.

There is yet another parallel to be drawn between the character of the city and the experience of the people of God in Philadelphia. "I will write upon him the name of my God," the promise continues, "and the name of the city of my God, the new Jerusalem, which cometh down out of heaven from my God, and mine own new name." The city of Philadelphia had by its own choice acquired a new name, *Neokaisareia*,

"New Caesar," in honor of Tiberius or Germanicus. (If the former, the comparison would be with Augustus; if the latter, it would be with Tiberius.) The new name was used for a while but fell into disuse, according to Ramsay, about A.D. 42–50. The promised reward to the faithful of the Philadelphia church sets the name of the true God in vivid contrast with the name of the Caesar who claimed to be a god. "I will write upon him the name of *my* God," emphasizes the authority of Jesus Christ to bestow upon his faithful followers the designation "children of my Father." God is the God of Jesus Christ. The name corresponds with the name "City of God" or "the new Jerusalem." Conferred by Christ upon the faithful, it serves as a guarantee that they are even now citizens of the heavenly city which is to be. Thus the Philadelphian Christians are assured that though they are citizens of an earthly city that once bore the name of a Caesar who claimed to be a god, they are in fact citizens of the new Jerusalem bearing the new name of the God of Jesus Christ.

The Christians of Philadelphia, like their brethren at Smyrna, had been forced to endure a trial at the hands of the Jewish population. Doubtless these were Jewish nationalists who deeply resented the inroads made in their ranks in earlier years by the Christians. Their distaste for Christians was sharpened by the tendency of the Roman authorities and the pagans to identify them with the Christians. At this period the rift between the synagogue and the church was complete, at least in the province of Asia. The wealth and power of the Jewish communities did nothing to soften the feeling of the poorer Christians toward the Jews. "Behold, I give of the synagogue of Satan, of them that are Jews, and they are not, but do lie" means "I am delivering up" these Jews (who had evidently persecuted the Christians). In some way these Jews are to be compelled to recognize that the Christians are loved of Christ and are the true Jews.

In the face of impending trial, the church at Philadelphia is urged to "hold fast that which thou hast, that no one take thy crown." In the case of Philadelphia the crown was won and in possession of the faithful. In the case of Smyrna the crown was yet to be won. But it is likely that the author means to say that Philadelphia has won "title" to the same crown of life which waits as a reward for the faithful of Smyrna.

Laodicea: the church that was neither cold nor hot.—3:14–22

Laodicea is the one church of the seven concerning which no good thing is said. Even to Sardis, the church which had a name to live and was dead, it could be said, "But thou hast a few names in Sardis that did not defile their garments." Laodicea's outstanding characteristic, lukewarmness, has remained through the centuries as the classic example of that quality which is most despised among the churches of Christ. The indictment, "Thou art neither cold nor hot," has left upon Laodicea a mark of opprobrium that can never be erased. But there is one circumstance connected with the melancholy state of this church which produced for succeeding generations an unforgettable portrait of the living Christ of the churches. It is of the Christ standing outside a closed door knocking and wistfully appealing for entrance. For this and the beloved and memorable words, "Behold, I stand at the door and knock: if any man hear my voice and open the door, I will come in to him, and will sup with him, and he with me," we are in a sense indebted to the lukewarm saints of the Laodicean community. However greatly we may deplore the sin of indifference which threatened the life of this church, we may be grateful for the fact that it called forth this tender and appealing picture of the exalted Christ standing before a door that is closed and asking for entrance. It is a picture that speaks more eloquently than scores of sermons of the great grace of God.

Laodicea was not only lukewarm, the church had become infected with the love of material things. It may be described as the "poor rich church." This places it in striking contrast with Smyrna, which was the "rich poor church." Smyrna was

61

poor in this world's goods but rich in the things of the Spirit. Laodicea was rich in the things of the world but poor in the things of the Spirit. The material security of the Laodicean congregation had robbed these Christians of their sense of dependence upon God. Though rich, these Laodiceans were wretchedly poor. But the tragedy of their condition was that they were unaware of their spiritual poverty. They are told: "Because thou sayest, I am rich, and have gotten riches, and have need of nothing; and knowest not that thou art the wretched one and miserable and poor and blind and naked: I counsel thee to buy of me gold refined by fire, that thou mayest become rich, etc."

The case of Laodicea illustrates vividly the peril of money and materialism, which have the effect of blinding the eyes of the spirit of man. The result is that he who is blinded knows not that he is blind, nor is he capable of seeing and appropriating the realities of the Spirit. Poverty in material things is not always a blessing and is certainly not requisite to spiritual health; but it can be a blessing. It is not as difficult for one who is poor in this world's goods to recognize his dependence upon God as for the person who is economically secure. The peril of material wealth is always that it brings to one a false sense of security. Perhaps it would be more correct to say that it brings to one a sense of a security that is misplaced. Ultimate security is in God, but it is this that is difficult for the man who is rich in this world's goods to see. Laodicea is an example of a peril which constantly confronts the churches—a peril against which Christendom must ever be on guard: the love of money. Many modern churches might well take heed from the warning to Laodicea.

The Laodicean Christians had fallen victims to their environment. Laodicea was a manufacturing city. The soft wool produced in the valley of the Lycus was widely esteemed. Garments of various kinds were woven from this choice wool. The thriving trade had brought much wealth to the Christian community. Not far distant from Laodicea there stood the temple of the Phrygian god, Men Karou. There grew up a famous school of medicine in connection with this temple. Medicines manufactured in and around Laodicea were widely used. One of these was an ointment for the ears, another a powder for the eyes. The Laodiceans would understand the exhortation to buy "eyesalve to anoint thine eyes, that thou mayest see."

Ramsay said that there was no other city whose spirit and nature were more difficult to describe than Laodicea. He believed that there were no extremes in the character of the city and that "The City of Compromise" was an apt description. It was a city of bankers, traders, and financiers, easily adaptable to the needs and demands of others, pliable and accommodating. The church might easily have taken on the character of the community and become "the church of compromise," the church that was neither cold nor hot.

The lukewarmness of Laodicea brings forth the threat of being spewed forth from the mouth of Christ. The vivid symbolism strongly suggests the disgusting effects of the church's character. But the loving Christ offers Laodicea the opportunity he presents to all sickly members of his body—repentance and health. We cannot conclude from the picture of Christ at the door that he stands outside the door of the Laodicean church. The symbolism is hardly intended to convey this meaning. The lesson of the memorable picture is that Christ ever stands ready to come into human hearts when they are opened to him. The promise is rich in its suggestiveness of reward. Christ promises that he will enter an opened door and will sit down and sup with him who opens; and there is added the significant words, "and he with me." This is an assurance of intimate fellowship with Christ, of a close reciprocal relationship in which the believer shares fully the honor and responsibility of a common experience. Great honor is reserved for him who welcomes Christ and fights the good fight of faith. "He that overcometh, I will give to him to sit down with me in my throne, as I also overcame, and sat down with my Father in his throne." The faithful believer shares fully in the victory of Christ. Christ conquered death and ascended the throne. He who "overcometh," that is, he who is faithful in the midst of persecution and temptation, will share the honor and the glory of Christ's reign. This is not a promise of a reward to be realized only after death and the judgment; it is a promise of victory with Christ in this life through identification with him in his life, death, and resurrection. This prospect of victory and glory with the risen Christ offers a sharp contrast to the drab experience of Christians who were merely lukewarm. It speaks eloquently of the failure of riches and a spurious security to produce more than an experience that gave to a church a name that has never been forgotten—"neither cold nor hot."

Attributes of the Exalted Christ

In the seven letters to the churches, Christ is revealed in majesty and glory, the risen, exalted, and reigning Christ. Seven great characteristics are given as belonging to him. These may be illustrated as follows:

1. *His authority over the churches and his presence among them.*—"These things saith he that holdeth the seven stars in his right hand, he that walketh in the midst of the seven candlesticks" (Letter to Ephesus, 2:1).

2. *The Risen Christ, the Victor over death.*—"These things saith the first and the last, who was dead and lived *again*"— or, better, "came to life" (Letter to Smyrna, 2:8).

3. *The Christ who is the Word of God.*—"These things saith he that hath the sharp two-edged sword" (Letter to Pergamum, 2:12). (See 19:13,15, where it is said, "His name is called the Word of God," and "Out of his mouth proceedeth a sharp sword.")

4. *The Son of God.*—"These things saith the Son of God, who hath his eyes like a flame of fire, and his feet are like unto burnished brass" (Letter to Thyatira, 2:18).

5. *The Christ who is revealed in the Holy Spirit.*—"These things saith he that hath the seven Spirits of God, and the seven stars" (Letter to Sardis, 3:1). The "seven Spirits of

God" refers to the Holy Spirit, as is shown by the reference to the Trinity in 1:4–5, where the third member of the Trinity (that is, neither the Father nor the Son) is referred to as "the seven Spirits that are before his throne."

6. *The Messiah.*—"These things saith he that is holy, he that is true, he that hath the key of David, he that openeth and none shall shut, and that shutteth and none openeth" (Letter to Philadelphia, 3:7). (See the foregoing discussion concerning the letter to Philadelphia in which it is shown that "he that hath the key of David" is used here as a description of the Messiah.)

7. *The Perfect Witness and the Head of Creation.*—"These things saith the Amen, the faithful and true witness, the beginning of the creation of God" (Letter to Laodicea, 3:14). He is the *personal Amen* (Swete), by which it is indicated that his character guarantees his testimony. *Amen* means "verily" or "it is true." What our Lord spoke was validated in his life and character. He was the *true* or *perfect* Witness. Also he is styled here "the beginning of the creation of God." The Greek word is *archē,* "first" or "head." His pre-eminence over all created things is what is meant. The author does not think of Christ as the first of created beings in the sense that he was a part of the created order. The meaning is that he is over all created beings and things.

Sevenfold Reward to the Churches

The letters also give a series of promised rewards to the churches. There is a specific reward indicated for each church, but all the churches may share in each reward promised. Hence we may think of the series as a sevenfold reward in which all the churches may share if they are faithful to Christ. This may be illustrated in the following manner:

1. *The privilege of eating of the tree of life.*—"To him that overcometh, to him will I give to eat of the tree of life, which is in the Paradise of God" (Letter to Ephesus, 2:7). The tree of life is the symbol of the source of life. The tree of life is

found first in the garden of Eden (Genesis 2:9). Presumably it was the source of everlasting life. The first pair had the privilege of eating of this tree but lost the right to immortality upon the earth by eating of the tree of the knowledge of good and evil (Genesis 3:19). In Revelation the privilege of eating of the tree of life is a promise to believers of eternal life. Through the experience of union with Christ, the believer receives life that cannot be terminated by death.

2. *The right to wear the crown of life.*—"Be thou faithful unto death, and I will give thee the crown of life" (Letter to Smyrna, 2:10). There is an addition to the promise in verse 11. It is: "He that overcometh shall not be hurt of the second death." The second death is the final condemnation of the wicked. This is seen in 20:14: "And death and Hades were cast into the lake of fire. This is the second death, *even* the lake of fire. And if any was not found written in the book of life, he was cast into the lake of fire." The crown of life is the token of victory over this death which is given to all believers. He who wears this crown cannot be touched by the "second" death, which is reserved for the wicked and for death itself (Hades).

3. *The right to eat of the hidden manna and to possess the protection of the name of God.*—"To him that overcometh, to him will I give of the hidden manna, and I will give him a white stone, and upon the stone a new name written, which no one knoweth but he that receiveth it" (Letter to Pergamum, 2:17). The manna was a source of sustenance and life for the Israelites on their journey to the Promised Land. Faithful Christians are promised a life-giving experience here that will sustain them on their pilgrimage. Also, they are assured of the protection of the name of God. (See the reference to the name on the white stone in the foregoing discussion of the letter to the church at Pergamum.)

4. *The privilege of sharing in the rule and glory of Christ.*—"And he that overcometh, and he that keepeth my works unto the end, to him will I give authority over the nations: and he shall rule them with a rod of iron, as the vessels of the

potter are broken to shivers; as I also have received of my Father: and I will give him the morning star" (Letter to Thyatira, 2:26–28). This is a promise to the faithful of participation in Christ's reign. Nothing is to be denied those who are faithful to the end. Christ reigns at the right hand of God. He who is faithful until death comes will be given the high privilege of participating with Christ in his progressive victory over evil and in his sovereign reign as King of kings and Lord of lords. He will be the recipient of "the morning star," brightest and most beautiful luminary of the before-dawn heavens. The beautiful imagery is suggestive of the glory of the reward reserved for all faithful believers.

5. *The privilege of sharing in Christ's holiness.*—"But thou hast a few names in Sardis that did not defile their garments: and they shall walk with me in white; for they are worthy. He that overcometh shall thus be arrayed in white garments; and I will in no wise blot his name out of the book of life, and I will confess his name before my Father and before his angels" (Letter to Sardis, 3:4–5). The white garments are symbolic of the holiness that is reserved in heaven for the saints. Christ himself is arrayed in white, that is to say, he is spotless and undefiled by sin. The faithful believers may cherish as the prospect of reward the privilege of partaking of this perfect holiness of Christ. There are two other rewards closely related to the bestowal of Christ's holiness: the right of the believer to have his name kept in the book of life, and the honor of having his name confessed by Christ in the presence of the Father and his angels. The latter is in keeping with words of Jesus uttered in the days of his flesh. (See Matthew 10:32 and Luke 12:8.)

6. *Spiritual security and a place of honor in God's service.*—"He that overcometh, I will make him a pillar in the temple of my God, and he shall go out thence no more: and I will write upon him the name of my God, and the name of the city of my God, the new Jerusalem, which cometh down out of heaven from my God, and my own new name" (Letter to Philadelphia, 3:12). As was said in the discussion of the letter

67

to Philadelphia, the pillar in the temple of God here is a symbol of spiritual security. It is a figure which would appeal to the Philadelphians in the light of their experience with earthquakes. The place of the pillar, in the temple of God, is suggestive of a place of honor in God's service. The security of a settled abode is suggested by the promise, "He shall go out thence no more." The new name and the name of the New Jerusalem to be written upon the person of the faithful believers are to be understood, as was seen, against the background of the name of the new Caesar, which Philadelphia had once had. The reward here promised might well apply to the present life. Faithful Christians need not await death to claim the right to wear the name of their God and of the New Jerusalem. Paul taught that "our citizenship is in heaven" in writing to the Philippian saints (Philippians 3:20), a doctrine in keeping with the application to this life of the promised reward to the Philadelphian saints.

7. *Intimate fellowship with Christ and the honor of sharing his reign.*—"Behold, I stand at the door and knock: if any man hear my voice and open the door, I will come in to him, and will sup with him, and he with me. He that overcometh, I will give him to sit down with me in my throne, as I also overcame, and sat down with my Father in his throne" (Letter to Laodicea, 3:20–21). The beautiful symbolism stresses the intimacy of communion the faithful believer may enjoy with his risen Lord. When two persons sit down and eat together, a bond of intimacy is established. In Oriental countries the act of eating together is a test and sign of friendship. When one becomes host to another, he gives his guest the freedom of his house. When a believer becomes host to the risen Christ, he gives him full access to the home of his soul. Our Lord, according to this promise, awaits only the response to his knock and an opened door to bestow upon us the blessing of his presence. There is repeated here the promise of the faithful believer of sharing in Christ's reign as the Son who sits at the right hand of the Father. The reward is promised in another form in the letter to Thyatira.

THE GREAT DRAMA
of the
SOVEREIGNTY OF GOD

ACT ONE

God asserts His Sovereignty over the
World in Jesus Christ: The Court of
Heaven and the Breaking of the Seven
Seals.—Chapters 4–11.

✝

Scene One

THE VISION OF THE COURT OF HEAVEN

(Chapters 4–5)

THE great drama which is to be unfolded in a series of remarkable visions now begins. The beginning is magnificent in its conception and execution. As the curtain is drawn aside, we gaze upon the glories of the supramundane world, the incomparable majesty of God, the cosmic mystery of redemption. The opening scene sets the tone of the entire drama. The genius of the author and his splendid obedience to the sure guidance of the Spirit are wonderfully manifest here. His drama is to teach the sovereignty of God in Jesus Christ; all is to articulate this great theme. The source and certainty of the sovereignty of God are represented in the opening scene in unforgettable symbols and action. The remaining visions will be permeated with the spirit and truth of this wonderful scene.

As the curtain is drawn aside here, we gaze upon *the things which are*. The author, in giving his commission to write, had said that he had been told to "write therefore the things which thou sawest, and the things which are, and the things which shall come to pass hereafter" (1:19). God is eternal, Christ is eternal, the Lamb is the Lamb slain from the foundation of the world. The things revealed here do not belong to time; they have expressions in time, but they are above both time and space. They cannot belong to "the things which shall come to pass hereafter." This opening scene, therefore, fixes the character of the Revelation: the book unfolds a cosmic

73

drama. The drama belongs in part to history, but it is a mistake to limit it to history. Chronological schemes violate the purpose and spirit of the book. The author takes us upon a high mountain, as it were, and bids us peer into the mysteries of the infinite. The division between time and eternity, space and infinity, fade as the eyes of the Spirit are opened and the glories of the world of the Spirit are revealed. As the visions are unfolded, we realize that movement from the world of men and events to the world of spirit and back again becomes easy; almost imperceptibly the transfer is made. It is necessary for the reader to exercise spiritual imagination, faith, and poetic appreciation, therefore, as he follows the unfolding of the drama. Through these channels the Spirit can speak to make clear to the teachable the message of the book.

Revelation is a book of great theological ideas. At the very beginning of the great drama, we are brought face to face with the important religious ideas upon which all Christian theology is based. At once the reality of God, Christ, and redemption are set forth. These great ideas are not stated in Revelation in abstract terms as Paul would state them, but they are no less great theological ideas for this fact. They are presented in remarkable pictures and symbols. Instead of a statement that God is the great First Cause and Sovereign of the universe, we see him pictured in majesty upon a throne receiving the homage of the four and twenty elders and the four living creatures. There is no statement of the doctrine of redemption here, but there is given a picture of "a Lamb standing, as though it had been slain." A study of the theology of Revelation will reveal a consistency of the great doctrines of the book with the theological ideas of the remainder of the New Testament. This is significant in the light of the fact that Revelation is the only apocalypse in the New Testament and is so radically different in character from the other writings. The author of the Revelation begins with his theology where all Christian theology must begin: with God and redemption through the eternal Christ.

74

*The Throne of God, the Four and Twenty Elders, and
the Four Living Creatures.—Chapter 4*

The author enters in spirit the door of heaven to gain his
first great vision. He is told, "Come up hither, and I will show
thee the things which must come to pass hereafter." This is a
general introduction to all the visions that are to follow and
does not apply exclusively to the vision of the Court of
Heaven; for certainly God, Christ, and redemption cannot
be designated as "things which must come to pass hereafter."
By his statement, "Straightway I was in the Spirit," the author
lays claim to the inspiration of the Holy Spirit for his writing,
suggests the ecstatic nature of the experience from which his
visions came, and emphasizes the *spiritual* character of the
matters he is to reveal.

In the magnificent portrayal of God which follows, the
central teaching is *the sovereignty of God* over all the universe; and yet in the symbols other great characteristics are
suggested. The attributes of God revealed in this extraordinary vision are apparently seven in number and may be indicated as follows:

1. *God Is Spirit*—There is no actual description of God.
The author states that "there was a throne set in heaven, and
one sitting upon the throne; and he that sat *was* to look upon
like a jasper stone and a sardius." With all his capacity for
symbolism and anthropomorphism, the author does not
undertake to describe the Sovereign of all the universe; he
can only say he was *like*. Thus in his refusal to describe God
in anthropomorphic terms, the author leaves us with the
lesson that *God is Spirit*. In that he is Spirit, he is "completely
other" from man, unlimited by time or space and entirely
independent of the creative process of which he is the author.
The stones to which God is likened are noted for their beauty
and brilliance. The jasper stone is like crystal, and the sardius
is a reddish stone capable of flashing brilliance. The com-

parison of God in his nature to these stones suggests that the expression of his character is *glorious*.

2. *God Is the Eternal.*—"And *there was* a rainbow round about the throne, like an emerald to look upon." If the rainbow accents the magnificence of the Court of Heaven, it is also reminiscent of God's covenant with Noah. The rainbow served as a sign to Noah and his descendants that God would never again destroy man from the face of the earth by a flood of waters. The God of Noah is the God who now sits upon the throne of the universe as the Seer of Patmos faces the grave crisis of the threat of the imperial Roman power. The God of the old dispensation who loved and saved his people is the God of the New Testament. God is One, God is *eternal.* His rainbow has not been removed from the heavens.

3. *God Is Sovereign*—"And round about the throne were four and twenty elders sitting, arrayed in white garments; and on their heads crowns of gold." Why twenty-four elders? Perhaps they represent the twelve patriarchs of the old dispensation and the twelve apostles of the new. There may be here an echo of the promise of Jesus to the twelve: "Ye also shall sit upon twelve thrones, judging the twelve tribes of Israel" (Matthew 19:28). Each of the elders wears a crown and is, therefore, a king in his own right. At stated intervals "the four and twenty elders shall fall down before him that sitteth on the throne, and shall worship him that liveth for ever and ever and shall cast their crowns before the throne saying, Worthy art thou, our Lord and our God, to receive the honor and the power: for thou didst create all things, and because of thy will they were, and were created." By the remarkable symbolism is emphasized the fact that God is *Sovereign,* the *Great King over all.* These elders are kings, but they gladly and obediently cast their crowns before the Great King who sits upon the throne.

The blasphemous claim of an earthly ruler such as the Emperor Domitian to be divine fades into puny insignificance against this extraordinary representation of the sovereignty of

God. The Christians of the Province of Asia would not fail to grasp this truth and would be greatly heartened by it.

4. *God Is Power.*—"And out of the throne proceed lightnings and voices and thunders." The vast, unlimited power of God seems to be suggested here. Lightning and thunder are manifestations of great power in nature. And they are awe-inspiring. All the power of all the universe is concentrated in the throne of God. The very contemplation of this concentrated power is calculated to fill the reverent mind with awe and wonder.

5. *God Is Immanent in His Creation.*—"And there were seven lamps of fire burning before the throne, which are the seven Spirits of God." As we have learned, the "seven Spirits of God" is a designation in Revelation of the Holy Spirit. Seven represents perfection, so that the Holy Spirit is the *perfect* Spirit. And so, if we interpret correctly the author's symbolism here, we learn that, while God is the Great Sovereign of the universe, outside the creative process, he is also immanent in the world of human beings. He comes to his people in the person of the Holy Spirit. Because he does visit his people, men of flesh and blood may have relations with him and may know him as the God and Father of Jesus Christ who truly revealed him.

6. *God Is Holy.*—"And before the throne, as it were a sea of glass like unto crystal." This sea of glass before the throne suggests the *unapproachableness* and *majesty* of God. He is unapproachable in his majesty because he is the Holy God before whom nothing defiled can appear. The brilliance of a glassy sea would blind the vision of men who approached the throne and make it impossible for them to look upon the glorious One whose person is the essence of holiness. The picture here and throughout is reminiscent of Isaiah's vision in the temple in which he was awed by the majesty that he saw. But it was the holiness of God which the vision most surely impressed upon the mind of the prophet. He heard the seraphim as they cried one to another, "Holy, holy, holy, is Jehovah of hosts: the whole earth is full of his glory"

77

(Isaiah 6:3). Isaiah was undone by his vision. The contemplation of God impressed upon him his own sinfulness in contrast with the holiness of God, and so he cries out, "Woe is me: for I am undone; because I am a man of unclean lips, and I dwell in the midst of a people of unclean lips: for mine eyes have seen the King, Jehovah of hosts" (Isaiah 6:5). The Seer of Revelation is faithful to the holy character of God as that character is revealed in Isaiah and in all the prophets.

7. *God Is the Source of All Life.*—"And in the midst of the throne, and round about the throne, four living creatures full of eyes before and behind. And the first creature was like a lion, and the second creature was like a calf, and the third creature had a face as of a man, and the fourth creature was like a flying eagle. And the four living creatures, having each one of them six wings, are full of eyes round about and within: and they have no rest day and night, saying, Holy, holy, holy is the Lord God, the Almighty, who was and who is and who is to come."

The symbolism of the four living creatures is drawn from the vision of Ezekiel, which is described in chapter 1 of his prophecy. The song of the creatures is an echo of the song of the seraphim in the vision of Isaiah. The four living creatures are apparently representative of all living beings. The lion is thought of as the king of wild beasts, the calf (or the ox) is representative of the domestic animals, the man is the crown of creation, and the eagle is the most prominent of the birds of the air. Thus all the important beings of the animal creation are represented in the four living creatures which may be interpreted as a composite representative of all beings that have life. These are ever before the throne of God, as it were, where the source of all life resides. The chief function of the four living creatures is to worship him who sits upon the throne. Thus do they acknowledge God as the creator and sustainer of life. In this worship of the four living creatures, the whole created order of beings joins, for they represent all things that breathe before him who is the author and sustainer of life.

78

The Roll of the Seven Seals, and Acceptance by the Lamb of Challenge to Open It.—Chapter 5

The action of the great drama now begins. The scene is still the Court of Heaven. God is still in the center of the stage, the Great Sovereign of the universe, seated in majesty upon his throne, surrounded by the four and twenty elders and the four living creatures. But now there comes upon the stage the Lamb. With unparalleled skill the artist paints the picture of his significance for the action of the entire drama. God has been given the central place in the drama; by the magnificent portrayal of his sublime majesty and glory, the theme of the great drama is unfolded from the beginning; God is the Great Sovereign, and there is no other god. But there is another great character of cosmic importance, another who shares with God the independence of time and space. He is the Lamb. With exceedingly skilful strokes the author brings the Lamb into exalted relationship with the Great One upon the throne; with consummate artistry he is identified with Jesus of Nazareth and is yet portrayed as the exalted Christ who has won redemption for all men. By the relation of the Lamb to the scroll in the right hand of God, he is brought into vital connection with all the action that is to follow.

The book which rests in the right hand of God should be thought of as a roll, or scroll, for it was such a "book" that the author saw in his vision. The roll was "close sealed" with seven seals, by which is meant it was securely sealed. The seal gave to a writing in ancient times the writer's imprimatur and assured its genuineness, and at the same time served as a warning to any who would open the document without authority. The roll was written "within and on the back." This was suggestive of the fact that it was "full" of writing.

And now the author sees himself as an actor in the great drama. He is a witness to the heavenly events; he hears the challenge of the strong angel to any who would dare to take the roll from the hand of God and break the seals so that the contents of the book might be made known; he weeps when it appears that there is no one in all the universe who is worthy to take the book from the hand of God. Surely there is significance in this identification of the prophet with these great cosmic events. God's prophet believes that he has a part in the drama. He knows that he is God's spokesman in the crisis that has fallen upon the churches. He realizes that if he is to speak with authority, he must have knowledge of the fountainhead of knowledge. He is a man, and not more than a man, but he is a man with a heavenly experience. He identifies himself with his brethren the prophets and knows he is one of them. Later on, when he is to fall down as if to worship the angel who "showed" him "these things," he will hear the angel say, "See thou do it not: I am a fellow-servant with thee and with thy brethren the prophets and with them that keep the words of this book: worship God" (22:9). The Seer of Patmos is one of the great company of prophets, then; but he is a prophet who refuses to stand aside in a time of crisis; rather he is one who struggles for vision; rather he is one who searches through tribulation for a message from God; rather he is one who determines that he shall have a message for his own time. And in revealing that message, he unabashedly claims that he has seen what others have not seen, he has heard what others have not heard. With sublime assurance he dares to picture himself as a witness to the events of a cosmic drama taking place in the Court of Heaven. It is as if he intends to say: "I will speak in this hour of crisis; I have somewhat to say; I am God's man; I have had a heavenly experience, I have seen the vision glorious; my authority is based upon what I have seen and heard and felt; therefore, give heed to my message!"

If the prophet sees himself as a man, with a message from heaven, he unfailingly identifies himself with humanity and humanity's struggle. He declares that he "wept much, because no one was found worthy to open the book or to look thereon." Doubtless he felt that the mysterious roll contained truths that he needs must know as a prophet of God. His weeping reflects his sympathy with God's people and his sense of the tragedy of the world. He is capable of a broken heart. In this he meets one of the sure demands of a prophet of God. He who stands before the people to speak for God cannot speak the things of God unless his heart can be touched by the sorrows of men and the tragedy of the world. The Seer of Patmos is a true prophet here. And in his weeping he reveals the plight into which every true prophet must now and again fall. That plight is compounded of perplexity and doubt. Often it brings from the anguished lips of the prophet the cry, "Why, oh God, why?" John was not dealing superficially with the problems of the crisis of his time. Patmos had been no delusion. Through tears and sweat he had been compelled to search for the meaning of the mysteries of God's providence. His hands were calloused by hard labor in the mines, and all the while he carried upon his heart the burden of the churches.

Those of us who also yearn to speak for God do not have great difficulty in placing ourselves in the position of the Seer of Patmos. We, too, have been perplexed; we, too, have longed for a knowledge of the mysteries of Providence; we, too, have "wept much."

The prophet of Revelation was rewarded for his weeping. One of the elders came forward with the command, "*Stop weeping.*" (It is in this manner that the Greek presents the elder's command.) There is One who possesses authority to take the roll from the hand of God and break its seals. He is the Lion of the tribe of Judah, the Root of David. By this the prophet is assured that Christ holds the key to the mysteries contained in the roll and that he has won the right to reveal these mysteries and interpret them. Thus does he learn of the exalted part that Christ must play in the unfolding of this great drama of the sovereignty of God. Thus does he learn that God's prophet must accept the assistance of Christ in his search for the meaning of the mysteries.

The Christ who has authority to break the seals of the roll and reveal its contents is the "Lion that is of the tribe of

Judah, the Root of David." By this designation he is identified as the Messiah of Israel. In the prophecy concerning his sons, Jacob had called Judah "a lion's whelp" (Genesis 49:9). The founder of the tribe was called a lion, and now the name is applied to the greatest of all the members of the tribe, Jesus. The figure of the lion presents him as the great One of the tribe, for the lion is the king of beasts. He is also called the "Root of David," by which he is identified as the Messiah who sprang from the house and lineage of David. Isaiah had prophesied, "And there shall come forth a shoot out of the stock of Jesse, and a branch out of his roots shall bear fruit" (11:1). The shoot or sapling springing from a root had become one of the well-known figures of the Messiah.

By this designation of Christ as the Lion of the tribe of Judah and the Root of David, Christ is grounded in history. John sees him as the exalted Christ in the Court of Heaven. But the course of his earthly life is by no means forgotten; indeed, the earthly experience of Christ has become part and parcel of his character. The human Jesus and the heavenly Christ are one. The Root of David who lived his life as a man and who fulfilled his destiny as the Messiah of Israel is the heavenly being before whom as the Lamb of God the four and twenty elders will fall in worship and in whose honor the ten thousand times ten thousand will sing.

The Lion is also the Lamb. It is as a Lamb "as though it had been slain" that the Christ steps forth in the throne room of God to take from the hand of the Great King the roll of the seven seals. And herein is the great paradox of redemption dramatically portrayed. It is the paradox of the cross. The lamb is a symbol of weakness and innocence. Though Jesus of Nazareth was the Lion of the tribe of Judah, the great One of this tribe, and the greatest of all the sons of men, he was the Lamb who in weakness and innocence endured the shame of the cross and died the death of the wicked. The death he died was abject defeat and stark tragedy. But it was the manifestation of redemptive love; and redemptive love breaks the confines of death to fashion victory out of defeat.

Through redemptive love God made the cross and the shed blood of the Lamb the means of redemption. And in this manifestation of redemptive love there was released in history the greatest power that humanity can know. The Lamb is, therefore, the symbol of power—vast spiritual power— power that no earthly power can destroy. The Lamb in his weakness—the weakness of the cross—is the source of the creative, healing, redeeming power of love in the world: love among men, love in the affairs of men, love cleansing sinners and making of unregenerate beings children of God, love saving civilization from decay, love moving redeemed men ever higher in their pilgrimage toward the City of God. Such love is indestructible. John saw it so in his day. The Lamb in his weakness stands over against the might of the Caesar and the crushing power of imperial Rome. But the Seer of Patmos staked his all on the Lamb, knowing that redemptive love cannot be destroyed, knowing that the power of the Cross would bring victory for the children of God.

The Lamb stands for us in a world cursed by the power of the atomic bomb and by human inventions more potent for destruction by far than were the legions of ancient Rome. But the power of the cross has not been destroyed, and the cross cannot be removed from history. It is still the wellspring of regenerative, healing, redemptive love. The Lamb is alive. We who stand with him in our day of crisis should not forget his meaning for the Seer of Patmos in his day of crisis. We must have faith, as John had faith, in the power of redemptive love to survive every assault of material, demonic power. But we must live with the Lamb to live. We must know him as the Jesus of history—the Lion of the tribe of Judah and the Lamb slain from the foundation of the world—if we would live in an era that ushers in the age of atomic power. We must obey his teachings given as he walked among men, and we must embrace his love as the Lamb of God if we are to enjoy the healing of the stream that had its rising in Calvary.

As if to accent this truth concerning the Lamb, John uses the symbolism of his seven horns, which represent his perfect power, and the seven eyes, which, it is explained, are the "seven Spirits of God, sent forth into all the earth." His power is available to men, for he is present among men in the Holy Spirit. The symbolism teaches us that Christ and the Holy Spirit are inseparable. The seven Spirits of God—the Holy Spirit—are "sent forth into all the earth." The Holy Spirit brings Christ as a living Christ to men. He came from the risen, exalted Christ at Pentecost to bring back Jesus to the one hundred and twenty. He performed his work on the basis of the work of the man Jesus. The deposit which Jesus of Nazareth had left in the lives of the disciples was ignited into a living flame by the return of the *risen* Christ in the person of the Holy Spirit. The function of the Holy Spirit is to make Jesus Christ alive and real to all who will receive him. And there can be no separation of the work of the Holy Spirit from the work of Jesus of Nazareth. This work of the man Jesus is the basis upon which the Holy Spirit inspires and guides to the knowledge of truth.

Dramatically the Lamb takes the roll from the hand of God. The act is the signal for a great chorus of praise from the four and twenty elders and the four living creatures. In their song the elders and the four living creatures reveal the basis of the Lamb's authority to break the seals of the roll. It was that he had by his death redeemed from the race of men a peculiar people: "and madest them to be unto our God a kingdom and priests; and they reign upon the earth." The redeemed have been made a kingdom; that is, a royal people. There is here an echo of the words of Jehovah to the children of Israel, "And ye shall be unto me a kingdom of priests, and a holy nation" (Exodus 19:6).

The reign of this royal people is *upon the earth,* and it is a present reign. The correct reading, "they reign," may be rendered "they are reigning." In any event the words here stress the actual and present reign of the people of God upon the earth as a result of the redemptive work of Jesus Christ. It is unnatural to refer this statement to a future reign of the saints, or, as R. H. Charles does, to interpret it as "proleptic"

84

and as applying primarily to the "millennial kingdom" in chapter 20.[1] The statement is highly significant for the proper interpretation of "kingdom" and "reign" in the book of Revelation and for the right application of the book to the present world order.

The act of the Lamb in taking the roll is the signal for a mighty chorus of praise from all created things in the universe. The chorus is begun by "ten thousand times ten thousand" and is taken up by "every created thing which is in heaven, and on the earth, and under the earth, and on the sea, and all things that are in them." In the final chorus the Lamb and the Great Sovereign of all are praised together: "Unto him that sitteth on the throne, and unto the Lamb, *be* the blessing, and the honor, and the glory, and the dominion, for ever and ever." To this the four living creatures said, "Amen." "And the elders fell down and worshipped."

[1] *The Revelation of St. John, I.C.C.,* Vol. I, p. 148.

Scene Two

THE BREAKING OF THE SIX SEALS:
"HISTORY'S PAGEANT OF SUFFERING"

(Chapter 6)

THE action of the great drama proceeds as the Lamb takes the roll from the hand of God and begins to break the seals one by one. As each seal is broken, John is permitted to see a vision depicting some mysterious incident or series of incidents. Each vision is intended to convey some truth or give some warning of significance. The question arises as to what the contents of the roll mean and what interpretation is to be given to the visions that come in connection with the breaking of the seals.

It is obvious that the revelations that are made under the breaking of the seals are designed to convey truth which is interpreted by Christ. The Lamb breaks the seals; whatever is revealed by the breaking of the seals is truth which Christ permits to be known. Clearly its revelation is intended to be helpful. Certainly what is revealed by Christ should give comfort to the Seer and to his readers in the crisis faced by the churches.

It is not correct to think of the roll as containing "decrees," as if with the breaking of the seals certain events and actions in history are thereby permitted. The roll contains an account of facts of history but not decrees which determine that certain events shall take place. Nor are we to look upon the breaking of the seals as revealing a chronological chart of history, nor of succeeding ages or eras in history. The visions given under the breaking of the seals are designed to help the people of God to place the proper estimate upon certain facts and incidents of history in their relation to the gospel of Jesus Christ and the sovereignty of God. It should be observed that the entire action, beginning with the breaking of the seals, leads up to the grand climax of the first act of the drama. This is found in the closing scene and is brought forward under the breaking of the seventh seal and the seventh trumpet blast, where this grand proclamation is made: "The sovereignty over the world is become [or became] our Lord's and his Christ's; and he shall reign forever and ever" (11:15). Now all that intervenes between the breaking of the first seal and this grand proclamation must be understood and interpreted in the light of this assertion of the sovereignty of God over the world in Christ. This leads us to insist that the visions under the breaking of the six seals, together with those under the series of the six trumpets, set forth problems for the people of God that are to be interpreted in the light of the fact of God's sovereignty. It is as if Christ through the Spirit were saying to his people: "Here are great disturbing facts of history: conquest, war, plague, death; and here is the obstinacy of man in his refusal to repent despite the recurring manifestations of the wrath of God. But here, above all, is the reality of the rule of God in his Son Jesus Christ. Interpret all in the light of this fact."

This approach to the problem of the contents of the roll in the hand of God leads us to designate the breaking of the six seals "History's Pageant of Suffering." By this designation it is meant to suggest that we are dealing in these visions with some of the great problems of history as they are to be interpreted and dealt with in the light of the gospel. If it seems that no answer appears as a solution of these problems as they are presented, let it be remembered always that the author's scheme of tying in the breaking of the six seals with the sounding of the seventh trumpet is his way of saying that the ultimate answer to all these problems is the sovereignty of God in Jesus Christ.

87

As a practical help to an understanding of the meaning of the visions under the first four seals, it is to be remembered that the destruction of Jerusalem had taken place in A.D. 70, twenty-five years prior to the writing of the Revelation. Josephus the Jewish historian claims that one million one hundred thousand people lost their lives in the siege and destruction of the city. Allowing for exaggeration in his estimate, it is nevertheless true that this was a holocaust which had profound influence upon Christian thinking in the latter part of the first century. Its terrors would be remembered by Christians and Jews alike. But it is to be remembered also that the history of the Jewish people was an open book to the Christian communities, which had in their possession the Greek translation of the Old Testament Scriptures and of the Apocryphal books. The latter contained the history of the Maccabean period describing the sufferings of the Jews under the Syrian kings. The non-Jewish Christians needed no Jewish history to remind them, however, that conquest, war, famine, and death were common to their world, even though there was at the time a temporary era of peace as a result of the unity and power of the Roman Empire. Also the reader is not to forget that the burning of Rome and the persecution of the Christians by the infamous Nero had left an indelible impression upon the minds of the Christian communities. The nature of the visions under the breaking of the seals is doubtless colored by all these facts and may be the better understood by acquaintance with them.

The First Four Seals: the Four Horsemen.—6:1-8

The four horsemen who appear under the breaking of the first four seals represent Conquest, War, Famine, and Death, in this order. These have been the scourge of mankind from early history. They appear and reappear in history in the order in which they appear in the visions here. The author's arrangement is thus a logical one. An individual appears in history who is fired by ambition to conquer the world; he must implement his conquest by war; war inevitably brings famine, and the issue of famine is death. These are hard, inescapable facts of history. John saw that these horsemen might ride again and that the struggling Christian communities might feel the cruel blows of their speeding hooves. But the hard facts of history are inescapable—the curtain must be pulled aside and the eyes of God's people must look upon the desolation wrought by the grim horsemen.

The first rider "came forth conquering, and to conquer." And it is said, "there was given unto him a crown." He is therefore rightly named "Conquest." He sat on a white horse, and carried a bow in the manner of the Parthian invaders who often struck terror to the people of the ancient world. The first horseman represents any individual who sets out to conquer the world. He might represent Domitian, who set himself up as a god in opposition to the Lord God of hosts. Or he may stand in our own time for a Napoleon, a Hitler, or some would-be conqueror yet to come.

The second rider came forth riding upon a red horse. To him it was given "to take peace from the earth, and that they should slay one another: and there was given unto him a great sword." Correctly this horseman is designated "War." The inevitable corollary of conquest is war. The conquerer, to make himself master, must make war.

The third rider is "Famine." He rides a black horse and holds in his hand a balance. A voice is heard crying out, "A measure of wheat for a shilling [a *denarius*, in value about seventeen cents], and three measures of barley for a shilling; and the oil and the wine hurt thou not." The symbolism suggests the scarcity of food. The rider holds a balance to weigh carefully the grain that is rationed. A "measure" of wheat equals approximately one quart of wheat, and this is worth a *denarius*, which was the standard wage for a day's labor. Barley is cheaper; and three quarts of this poorer grain may be obtained for a *denarius*. The oil and the wine are rare and precious and are not to be "hurt." This is a picture of famine that follows in the wake of war. Such famine, and

worse, we have seen in our own time as a result of World War
II, brought on by the ambitions of a man who wished to rule
the world.

The name of the fourth rider is "Death." He rides upon a
horse that was "pale" in appearance, or, as the Greek has it,
"pale green." Hades followed with the rider Death, which
is by way of saying "death followed death." To these two,
Death and Hades, was given "authority over the fourth part
of the earth, to kill with sword, and with famine, and with
death, and by the wild beasts of the earth." The work of the
fourth rider is the consummation of the work of the three
horsemen who have preceded him. The possibility that this
rider Death might appear in devastating power, as indicated
in the vision, in connection with the rising tide of persecution
or the appearance of a ruler who would fill the role of Antichrist, was in the mind of John. But this horseman always
rides, as he has ridden in our own time, when Conquest,
War, and Famine set forth before him on their missions of
destruction.

The Fifth Seal: the Martyrs.—6:9–11

The breaking of the fifth seal presents another problem in
"History's Pageant of Suffering." It raises the question as to
why the people of God must die at the hand of evil rulers.
The author in his vision sees underneath the altar "the souls
of them that had been slain for the word of God, and for the
testimony which they held." The altar is the altar before the
throne of God in heaven. These who have died in the cause
of Christ cry out, "How long, O Master, the holy and true,
dost thou not judge and avenge our blood on them that dwell
on the earth?" The author gives evidence here of his realism.
He does not deal lightly with the problems of injustice,
suffering, and death as they affect God's people. He does not
gloss over the fact that God's people do suffer and die with
no other crime to their charge but that they were loyal
to the cause of Christ. The author propounds no superficial

philosophy centered in a shallow optimism that "everything will turn out all right." He knows that the people of God must face the stern realities of persecution and death. Some, like Antipas at Pergamum, had given their lives because of their fidelity to the gospel. Scores had died as torches to light up Nero's gardens. Others would die. What, then, of the unjust persecution and the death by martyrdom of the people of God? John hears them as they cry out for the avenging of their blood. What is the answer? Recompense to the enemies of God's people will come in due time. At that time "the altar" will say, "Yea, O Lord God, the Almighty, true and righteous are thy judgments" (16:7). But there is even recompense now for the martyrs themselves. First, they are safe from all harm; they are "underneath the altar," close to the throne of God. Again, there is given to each one a white robe. In this is symbolized the holiness and purity they have won from God because of their loyalty unto death. Yet again, they are assured that they have blood brothers upon the earth who are prepared to make the supreme sacrifice, even as they have made it: "and it was said unto them, that they should rest yet for a little time, until their fellow-servants also and their brethren, who should be killed even as they were, should have fulfilled *their course.*" Thus it is indicated that the martyrs in heaven are one with the martyrs-to-be upon the earth; thus is dramatically illustrated the solidarity of the long line of saints, living and dead, who have loved not their lives unto death. To be in this line and to be one of this dying but deathless company is recompense and honor and glory!

The Sixth Seal: the End of the Age.—6:12–17

The end of the existing order of things seems to be in the mind of the author in the vision that is given under the breaking of the sixth seal. In his projection of "History's Pageant of Suffering," he reckons the end of time and history as one of the problems to be contemplated in relation to the gospel. Placed as it is with these other problems of history, the end of time and history is to be conceived of as an ever-present possibility. Hence, its reality is always projected from the future into the present. This lively sense of the end which characterized the thinking of first century Christians is the proper eschatological outlook of Christian theology. Such an outlook makes the end a part of the present. By this interpretation the consummation colors the present, and the end is not merely a temporal matter but becomes a dynamic of life in the kingdom of God. It was such an interpretation that Jesus made in his teaching concerning the *Parousia* and the end of the age. His emphasis was not upon "times and seasons" but upon life in the kingdom of God, colored by the end.

It is hardly profitable to attempt to analyze the author's ideas as to what the actual occurrences would be in connection with the end of the age. Perhaps he conceived of an actual dissolution of the natural order. His language would seem to imply this. And yet we must remember that he uses figurative language throughout and therefore we should not be too quick to press for a literalistic meaning here in the vision of the sixth seal. The apocalyptic symbols which he uses do suggest the consummation of the age, however; though not necessarily the consummation at an immediate date. The vision, as we have indicated, presents the end as a fact of history and as a problem to be reckoned with in the light of the gospel and the sovereignty of God in Jesus Christ. In this vision "the sun became black as sackcloth of hair, and the whole moon became as blood; and the stars of the heaven fell unto the earth, as a fig tree casteth her unripe figs when she is shaken of a great wind. And the heaven was removed as a scroll when it is rolled up; and every mountain and island were moved out of their places." Great cosmic disturbances are indicated by this imagery. That the author foresees the end of the age is emphasized in his vivid picture of judgment which follows. The multitudes of all classes who hide themselves in the caves and in the rocks of the mountains cry out to the mountains and to the rocks, "Fall on us, and hide us from the face of him that sitteth on the throne, and from the wrath of the Lamb: for the great day of their wrath is come; and who is able to stand?" This is manifestly a picture of the great final day in which God is to execute judgment upon sinners. This day is associated in the New Testament with the consummation of the age.

It is not so difficult in these times as formerly to think in terms of the end of history. Scientists have turned evangelists to warn us of the possibility of the destruction of civilization through the misuse of atomic power. But before the arrival of the atomic age, astrophysicists like Sir James Jeans had pointed out the possibility of some cosmic accident that would destroy our earth. We are taught by astronomy that our star, the sun, is slowly dying; so that, accident or no accident, the end of the world is a certainty, even according to the known facts of science. We are assured that while our earth is approximately three billion years old, it may continue to support life for an additional ten billion years, barring a cosmic accident, such as the entry of a wandering star into our solar system or the exploding of our star, the sun. These astronomical estimates as to the age of the earth and the future of our planet leave us with little or no consciousness that the end has any meaning for us. The possibility that our earth may be the victim of a cosmic accident makes some slight impression upon our imaginations, but neither this possibility nor the certainty that our earth will die when the energy of the sun has been dissipated has any ethical meaning aside from religion. What we are saying is that the end of the cosmic order actually has no meaning for the human race without the help of a cosmology that takes God into account.

For the non-Christian, the end has no meaning for life and personality—it is merely the end. Confronted with the possibility that the world might end in his lifetime, the average non-Christian would doubtless shrug his shoulders and give utterance to the commonly used slang, "So what?" Jesus, Paul, and the early Christian thinkers could not so easily

93

dispose of the end of history. To them it was a problem to be reckoned with. They saw the end as an event belonging to God's great economy, an event to be incorporated into the whole of God's dealings with the human race. It was an event to be related to the ongoing of God's purpose in history, an event to infuse the life of men in the present with ethical and moral attributes in keeping with the content of the end. The end, in the thinking of these men, would of necessity be accompanied by the judgment of God; therefore, the judgment must be so interpreted as to affect men's lives as they lived them out in the historical process. The end, therefore, becomes, in Christian theology, not merely a temporal event, but a consummation—"a divine event toward which the whole creation moves." Thus history is made purposive, for it moves toward the grand conclusion. The end contains God's justification of all he has done in history, the validation of all truth revealed through history, the vindication, above all, of Jesus Christ and the gospel. Thus, for the Christian individual and the Christian society, the end contains the validation of faith. Now "we walk by faith," now we gamble our lives on the grand assumption that God is and that the life everlasting is true; at the end we shall discover that we were right. Christian thought lays hold of this assurance and incorporates it into the gospel's interpretation of time and history. Thus is the consummation invested with meaning.

John was unaware of the scientific implications of his thesis concerning the end, but he saw with an eye of spiritual clarity that the gospel must reckon with the end. Boldly therefore he lays hold upon the fact of the end and in apocalyptic language presents it among the problems of "History's Pageant of Suffering." That the problem belongs to the realm of suffering appears from the cries of those who call for the mountains and the rocks to fall upon them. In so far as the problem of suffering at the end of history or in the persecution immediately confronting the churches is related to the lives of Christians, it is answered in part by the visions of the seventh chapter which immediately follow.

Scene Three

PRELUDE TO THE BREAKING OF THE SEVENTH SEAL

(Chapter 7)

IN swift succession the six seals of the roll have been broken, and in the visions which the opening of them unfolded we shared with John his struggle with the problems of "History's Pageant of Suffering." The seventh seal is yet to be broken. With dramatic skill the author pauses in the recital of the breaking of the seals before the mystery of the seventh seal is revealed. Before the action unfolding the secrets of the roll is resumed, he will consider the state of the people of God. If the four horsemen are to ride again; if other faithful saints are to shed their blood in the cause of Christ; if the end of history should come now or in the distant future, what shall be the fate of the people of God? Are there yet other struggles that God's people must endure as history proceeds apace? If the wrath of God should strike the enemies of God, can the people of God expect protection from its manifestation? These are the questions we now face with John as we approach this "interlude," or, perhaps more properly, this "prelude" to the breaking of the seventh seal.

The Sealing of the Servants of God.—7:1–8

The scene opens with "four angels standing at the four corners of the earth, holding the four winds of the earth,

95

that no wind should blow on the earth, or on the sea, or upon any tree." The picture is one of *restrained* destruction. The winds that came from the "corners" of the earth, that is, not from north, south, east, west, were thought by the ancients to be hurtful or destructive. Thus, the destruction which impends is held back. The reason for the restraining of destruction upon the earth is immediately apparent; before the earth becomes the scene of devastating forces, the people of God must be made safe. Their safety is assured by the placing of the "seal of the living God" upon their foreheads. John says, "And I saw another angel ascend from the sunrising, having the seal of the living God: and he cried with a great voice to the four angels to whom it was given to hurt the earth and the sea, saying, "Hurt not the earth, neither the sea, nor the trees, till we shall have sealed the servants of our God on their foreheads." There follows the account of the sealing of the one hundred and forty-four thousand, "out of every tribe of the children of Israel."

The question immediately arises as to the meaning of the one hundred and forty-four thousand. Is this a prophecy of the salvation of the Jews? Is this a reference to the people of Israel only?

It is difficult to see how the symbolism here can refer to Jews only. The author has made it clear that the sealing is of the "servants of our God." It is possible, of course, that he is describing in apocalyptic imagery here the safety of the Jews who have "come out from their tribes" to be the elect of God. If this be the correct view, this is a representation of the security of the "remnant" of Israel. But if the one hundred and forty-four thousand represents the "remnant" of Israel, it may as well represent the "remnant" and the Gentile Christians, who together make the New Israel of God. It is certainly possible to interpret the symbolism in this way, and it is in this way that we shall take it.

There seems to be no significance in the order in which the tribes are given here except the appearance of Judah at the head of the list. The reason for this is not far to seek: Christ was of the tribe of Judah. The implication in this fact is that, with Messiah and his tribe at the head of the list, the tribes would not refer exclusively to Jewish tribes, since the Messiah is Christ the Lord of Jews and Gentiles alike. The tribe of Dan is missing from the list—another suggestion that the author is not undertaking to employ a strictly Jewish pattern. The tribe of Levi is included, which is an irregularity, if the author intends to follow strictly the Old Testament pattern. The tribe of Levi was not assigned territory in Palestine when the Israelites were led into Canaan by Joshua. Another irregularity is the omission of the tribe of Ephraim since the tribe of Manasseh is included. Apparently "the tribe of Joseph" takes the place of Ephraim here. When the Israelites were settled in the Land of Promise, the tribes of Manasseh and Ephraim, taking the names of Joseph's sons, were both given allotments.

The one hundred and forty-four thousand represent, it is most reasonable to conclude, God's elect *upon the earth.* Sealed with the seal of God they are secure, not indeed from physical injury, but secure in the protection they have received for their immortal souls from the hands of God. The number one hundred and forty-four thousand (twelve times twelve) suggests completeness. Thus there is given in this vision encouragement and assurance for the Christians in their impending struggle with Rome and the Caesars. If the four horsemen should ride again, or if there should break forth upon the earth such plagues as the six trumpets of chapter 8 will herald, the people of God may rest in the assurance that no harm can come to their souls; they have been sealed with the seal of their God; in the contemplation, therefore, of violence, bloodshed, and death that may fall upon them, they may have no fear of what man may do unto them.

A Vision of the Eternal Blessedness of the Redeemed.—7:9–17

The scene changes from earth to heaven. The people of God who are caught in the forces of destruction while they live in the world are given, by the vision of the sealing of the one hundred and forty-four thousand, the assurance that their souls are beyond the power of the enemies of God to hurt. But now, in this magnificent vision of all the redeemed about the throne of God, they are granted added assurance. The lesson of this vision is that the *eternal salvation* of God's people is sure. The distinction between the one hundred and forty-four thousand and this "great multitude which no man could number" is not that the former are Jews only and the latter are "of every nation and of *all* tribes and peoples and tongues," but that the one hundred and forty-four thousand are the redeemed *upon the earth,* while this great multitude is all the redeemed of all time in heaven and in possession of their eternal reward. Thus, the author draws aside the curtain of eternity in this vision to reveal a picture of *eternal redemption.* By the aid of this vision the Christians who faced the wrath of the Emperor might keep before them their ultimate destiny, might see themselves in the vast throng about the throne of God.

The great multitude before the throne sings this song: "Salvation unto our God who sitteth on the throne, and unto the Lamb." The meaning of their song is that the salvation the redeemed possess is from God and the Lamb. Since God and the Lamb are the authors of the salvation the redeemed enjoy, no power in all the universe can destroy it. The multitude is arrayed in white robes, a symbol of their holiness. The Seer is asked, "These that are arrayed in the white robes, who are they, and whence came they?" When he defers to the Elder for the reply to the question, the Elder replies in a burst of poetic imagery that is surpassingly beautiful. Indeed, here we meet with one of the truly magnificent passages of all literature. The unforgettable answer of the Elder is:

> These are they that come out of the great tribulation, and they washed their robes, and made them white in the blood of the Lamb. Therefore are they before the throne of God; and they serve him day and night in his temple: and he that sitteth on the throne shall spread his tabernacle over them.

They shall hunger no more, neither thirst any more; neither shall the sun strike upon them, nor any heat: for the Lamb that is in the midst of the throne shall be their shepherd, and shall guide them unto fountains of waters of life: and God shall wipe away every tear from their eyes.

The "great tribulation" in this passage need not be limited in its reference to the tribulation connected with the consummation of the age. The words are certainly designed to give encouragement to the Asian Christians and their friends who faced martyrdom in the conflict of the churches with the Roman authorities. They are no doubt intended likewise to comfort the relatives and friends of Christians like Antipas of Pergamum who had already paid with their lives for their devotion to Christ. These martyrs who had died or were about to die were those *coming* (Greek, *erchomenoi*, present participle) out of the great tribulation. But if we go back to the picture of the numberless throng about the throne of God, we are impressed with the fact that this throng represents *all the redeemed of all time.* So great a multitude could hardly represent only those alive at the end of the age who passed through the tribulation of the last days. But each one of this vast multitude wears a white robe, and by the word of the elder we know that those arrayed in the white robes are those *coming* out of the great tribulation. By this reasoning "the great tribulation" is the earthly experience of the people of God—all the people of God. Therefore we have in these beautiful words a promise of the eternal redemption of all the people of God of all the ages.

What, then, may we who pass through the "great tribulation" of this earthly experience with its sufferings, struggles, sorrow, and death, gather by way of assurance from these words? We learn from them that our "white robes" that is, our righteousness or holiness, that which gives us the right to stand with the throng before the throne of God—were made white in the blood of the Lamb. Thus are we impressed with the place of grace in salvation. Plainly in this vivid picture the author leaves us with the lesson that we gain our right-

99

eousness and thereby our right to stand in the presence of the holy God, not by works, but through the redemptive work of Jesus Christ. Our author articulates in his own way the doctrine of salvation by grace.

Those whose robes have been washed in the blood of the Lamb are promised these rewards: (1) They are given the privilege of living and serving forever in the presence of God; they are before the throne, they serve him day and night in his temple, they are under the *shekinah* presence of the Almighty. God spreads his "tabernacle" over them (Greek, *skēnōsei*, literally, "will pitch his tent" over them). (2) They shall suffer no more from hardships imposed by nature—"They shall hunger no more, neither thirst any more; neither shall the sun strike upon them, nor any heat." (3) They shall enjoy contact forever with the source of life—the Lamb will be the Shepherd to guide them always "unto fountains of waters of life." (4) God himself will serve as their Great Comforter. He "shall wipe away every tear from their eyes."

The glorious experience depicted so beautifully in the words of the Elder centers in the *presence of God with his people*. The appeal of the promise lies in the prospect that those who have passed through "the great tribulation" and washed their robes in the blood of the Lamb shall actually live eternally with God.

Scene Four

THE BREAKING OF THE SEVENTH SEAL

(Chapters 8–9)

THE action set in motion by the breaking of the seals is now resumed. The dramatic prelude of chapter 7 has injected an air of suspense and expectancy into the movement and this is heightened by the effect produced by the actual opening of the seventh seal and the preparations which follow for the appearance of the seven trumpet angels. It is to be remembered that with the breaking of the seventh seal the action of Act One of the great drama is precipitated towards its grand climax in the great proclamation that is to be made with the seventh trumpet blast, for the series of seven trumpet angels belongs in its entirety to the opening of the seventh seal.

Breaking of the Seal and Preparation of the Seven Trumpet Angels.—8:1–6

The breaking of the seventh seal is made to stand out with extraordinary boldness, and the vast significance of this incident is dramatically portrayed by the simple statement that when the Lamb opened the seal, "there followed a silence in heaven about the space of half an hour." Up to this point the throne room of heaven has resounded with the worship of the elders and the four living creatures and has echoed with the praises of the redeemed and all created beings. It has presented a picture of ceaseless motion and life. But in the instant that the Lamb opens the seventh seal, all becomes still, and a vast silence falls upon the Court of Heaven. The hosts of heaven are transfixed and made speechless as they gaze raptly at the Lamb when he moves his hand to break the last seal of the roll that was taken from the hand of God. The deep silence continues for minute after minute as they contemplate in awe the effect of the Lamb's deed. For a full half hour the silence remains unbroken. Then the seven angels "that stand before God"—the angels of the Presence—are given each a trumpet, and movement begins again in heaven and the long silence is broken.

That which now transpires in the throne room of God is designed to show that the prayers of God's people upon the earth for succor have reached the throne of God and will be heeded. An angel pours incense upon the golden altar before the throne. In this action he is represented as "adding" to the prayers of the saints which were upon the altar. The smoke of the incense "went up before God," a symbol that the prayers of the saints are now known to God. The angel now fills his censer with fire from off the altar and casts the fire down to earth. In the coals that fall, the saints upon the earth have tangible evidence that their prayers to God have been heard. Thus are they assured that God is aware of their plight as they see coming upon the earth the plagues that are revealed under the sounding of the six trumpets.

The Sounding of the Six Trumpets: "The Tragedy of Unrepenting Humanity."—8:7–9:21

The strange plagues that now pass before our eyes are perhaps to be understood as pointing up to the lesson to be derived from the words at the conclusion of the final plague: "And the rest of mankind, who were not killed with these plagues [the fire and the smoke and the brimstone of 9:18], repented not of the works of their hands, that they should not worship demons, and the idols of gold, and of silver, and of brass, and of stone, and of wood; which can neither see,

102

nor hear, nor walk: and they repented not of their murders, nor of their sorceries, nor of their fornication, nor of their thefts" (9:20–21). Despite the vast suffering wrought by the five preceding plagues and now the death of "the third part of men" by this sixth plague, men refuse to repent of their wickedness and continue in their unbelief. It would appear, therefore, that these plagues have to do with "The Tragedy of Unrepenting Humanity." This interpretation receives support from the fact that the first four plagues are reminiscent of the Egyptian plagues which were sent by Jehovah to move Pharaoh to repentance but which actually did not effect repentance in the heart of the Egyptian monarch who held the children of Israel in bondage.

There is a limit upon the effect of these plagues. "A third part of the earth" is burned up; a "third part of the sea" becomes blood; the "third part of the sun" was smitten; the "third part of men" was killed, etc. These cannot be the so-called "plagues of the last days." It is reasonable to believe that plagues of the last days would be unlimited in their power to destroy. Apparently these plagues depict the continuous operation in history of the effects of sin and evil. They show how mankind forever suffers from his disobedience to God, and yet how in his blindness and rebellion he will not recognize the tragic results of his sin and refuses to repent.

The first four plagues have to do with devastation in nature and are strongly reminiscent of the plagues upon Egypt. The first is of hail and fire, mingled with blood. Its effect is the burning of "the third part of the earth," "the third part of the trees," and of "all green grass." The second plague comes because a great mountain burning with fire is cast into the sea, with the result that a third part of the sea becomes blood, a third portion of the living things of the sea die, and a third part of the ships are destroyed. With the sounding of the third trumpet, a great star falls from heaven upon the rivers and fountains of the earth causing them to become foul and bringing death to many men. The trumpeting of the fourth

103

angel brings a darkening of a "third part" of the sun, moon, and stars.

The sounding of the fifth trumpet to usher in the fifth plague is preceded by the vision of an angel flying in mid-heaven and "saying with a great voice, Woe, woe, woe, for them that dwell on the earth, by reason of the other voices of the trumpet of the three angels, who are yet to sound." By this device each vision appearing under the trumpeting of each of the three remaining angels is designated as a "woe." This applies even to the vision of the great proclamation of the seventh angel in 11:15. The proclamation of the reign of God in Christ is conceived of as a "woe" because of its meaning for the enemies of God.

When the fifth angel sounds, the Seer sees "a star from heaven fallen unto the earth." This star is Satan, for "he" has the key to the pit of the abyss, which he proceeds to open. Strange creatures called locusts come forth from the pit and proceed to torment men upon the earth who do not have the seal of God upon their foreheads. They do not have the power to kill but to cause intense suffering. Because of the torment of these creatures, "men shall seek death." But death will not come to them. The king of these terrible creatures is called in Hebrew Abaddon, and in Greek Apollyon; that is, De-stroyer. This plague is suggestive of the destructive, torment-ing power of sin. The work of the terrible creatures from the abyss is directed by the being called Destroyer. Only one group upon the earth is immune from the work of these evil creatures, and this group is the people of God—those who have the seal of God upon their foreheads. The Destroyer has no power over them; the evil creatures who do his bidding can-not torment them; they are secure from the devastation wrought in the souls of men by sin.

With the trumpeting of the sixth angel, "the four angels that are bound at the great river Euphrates" are loosed. These had been prepared "for the hour and day and month and year, that they should kill the third part of men." The releasing of these four angels is the signal for the mobilization

104

of a great army of horsemen, numbering "twice ten thousand times ten thousand." Fire and smoke and brimstone proceed from the mouths of the horses—"By these three plagues was the third part of men killed." This plague is reminiscent of Israel's captivity. It was from the region of the Euphrates, from Babylonia and Assyria, that her captors came. On many occasions the homeland of the Chosen People was overrun by cruel invaders, but the captivity remained the crowning blow to the nation in Old Testament times. Now these cruel horsemen of John's vision and their devastating work provide a dramatic figure of all captivity and suffering brought on by man's rebellion against God. But the tragic fact remains that, in spite of the captivity and the suffering and the death caused by man's sin and rebellion, those who survive the ravages of sin stubbornly refuse to repent. The melancholy conclusion of the matter is that the sum total of the wrath of God as symbolized in the plagues of the seven trumpets does not produce repentance in man: "The rest of mankind, who were not killed with these plagues, repented not of the works of their hands."

THE PROPHET AND THE EATING OF THE LITTLE BOOK

(Chapter 10)

THE six trumpets have sounded, and we await the blast of the seventh trumpet. Again the author exercises his dramatic skill to introduce an "interlude" which delays the execution of the expected action. It was so before the opening of the seventh seal, and it is true now as the reader expects the sounding of the final trumpet. At this point the consummation of the expected action is delayed, but there is skilfully introduced a vision which has the effect of heightening the drama. This vision of the prophet's eating the little book that was in the hand of the strong angel sharpens the emphasis upon the culmination of the action in the seventh trumpet blast. It is therefore more than an "interlude"; it serves to intensify expectation and interest in the great proclamation of 11:15.

Once again the Seer sees himself as an actor in the great drama. In the vision of the Court of Heaven, he had seen himself weeping because there was no one found worthy to take the scroll from the hand of God and break its seals. The book that he looked upon in that scene was the Lamb's book; only Christ was authorized to handle this scroll in the right hand of God. But now in this vision John sees himself in relation to a book that is his own. It is a little book (Greek, *biblaridion*) and is not to be confused with the roll of the seven seals. If John was an actor in the great cosmic drama as it was acted out in the Court of Heaven, he is even more an actor in the drama as he witnesses this great angel "coming down out of heaven" with the little book in his hand, for in this vision the Seer must take the book from the hand of the angel and eat it. Later he will again become a participant in the action as he obeys a command to "Rise and measure the temple of God."

Again there is revealed in the experience of the Seer of Patmos the demands to be met by the true prophet of God. John will persist in believing that he must play a part in the great drama; once more he refuses to stand aside. He is struggling for his message, and now as his vision moves on toward its grand climax, there is impressed upon him more clearly the character of the message he must proclaim and the demands it imposes upon the messenger. He reveals that in his vision he heard the great angel cry with a great voice and that then "the seven thunders uttered their voices." He was about to write, he declares, as the seven thunders uttered their voices, when he heard a voice from heaven saying, "Seal up the things which the seven thunders uttered, and write them not."

What is symbolized by the seven thunders? They suggest the echoes of the wrath of God which has been so forcibly impressed upon the author in the visions of the four horsemen and of the six trumpet angels. It would seem there had come to the author a temptation to major in the wrath of God; perhaps at this point he was moved to proceed with this theme. The time had now come for the prophet to face the implications for himself of a more comprehensive theme—a theme which involved an all-inclusive message. The Spirit is leading on toward the statement of this great message—a statement which will come when the seventh angel sounds his trumpet. Now the prophet must pause, take stock, and allow the Spirit to lead him into a soul-searching of himself before the greater revelation comes. Perhaps the prophet is even tempted by the seven thunders to bring his prophecy to a conclusion; in that case he would cease his work of writ-

107

ing with an incomplete message. But the last word has by no means been said, as the prophet discovers; and the last word is the best word, for it contains the completed "mystery of God, according to the good tidings which he declared to his servants the prophets." John obeys the command to "seal up the things which the seven thunders uttered." As a faithful prophet he will not stop with an incomplete message but will await the further revelation of the Spirit.

John hears in his vision a solemn oath from the lips of the angel. The angel "sware by him that liveth for ever and ever, who created the heaven and the things that are therein, and the earth and the things that are therein, and the sea and the things that are therein." The manner in which the oath of the angel is taken emphasizes the vast importance of that which he will now say. His words are: "There shall be delay no longer: but in the days of the voice of the seventh angel, when he is about to sound, then is finished the mystery of God, according to the good tidings which he declared to his servants the prophets." The solemn words of the angel point straight to the centrality and significance of the proclamation to be made when the seventh angel sounds. It is as if the reader were being told that this proclamation is the "sum and substance of the whole matter," that in it was to be found the heart of the message of the book of Revelation. The content of this proclamation and its significance will be considered in its proper place. Here let us briefly consider the words of the great angel.

The angel proclaims that there will be "delay" no longer. The Authorized Version renders the Greek word here by the English word "time." It is true that *chronos* does mean "time," but it may mean "delay," and here its natural meaning is "delay." By this statement it is indicated that there will be delay no longer in the revelation of the "finished" mystery of God. The mystery pertains to those events in history which led up to the birth of Christ. The mystery was "completed" in the coming of Christ and in his exaltation to the right hand of God to be King of kings and Lord of lords. The mystery was revealed to the prophets of the early Christian community when they grasped the fact that Jesus of Nazareth, the crucified, was indeed the Christ of God. This mystery was proclaimed by the earlier Christian prophets; now it will be proclaimed by John. In the range of his visions John looks into the past, the present, and the future. No chronological scheme limits him in the play of his imagination under the inspiration of the Spirit. The Spirit has taken him at this point to a point in time which is past—the finishing of the mystery of God in Christ. This takes place in "the days of the voice of the seventh angel," but the grand proclamation which is to be made is no new revelation; it was well known to the prophets at Pentecost; for under the inspiration of the Spirit they penetrated the "mystery" to discover that Jesus of Nazareth was Messiah and Lord. Thus, while the "days of the voice of the seventh angel" appear to be in the future, actually they are past. John will soon pass to the revelation of a vision which pertains to another great event of the past: the birth of the Messiah in chapter 12; and yet, in the manner that it is presented, it will appear to be a future event. In the same manner the "finishing" of the mystery of God, a past event, is cast into the future by the Seer's series of visions.

John is confident of his own place in the line of the prophets; he is conscious of the magnitude and relevance of his message; he knows that his message has come from God and that he can deliver it with the assurance that he speaks for God.

But the prophet must assimilate his message; he realizes that he and his message must be one. This is the lesson of the vision of the eating of the little book that he takes from the hand of the angel. "And I took the little book out of the angel's hand," he relates, "and ate it up; and it was in my mouth sweet as honey: and when I had eaten it, my belly was made bitter." The experience of Ezekiel is, of course, the prototype of John's experience here. The Old Testament prophet had been called to prophesy to a "rebellious house." Having been warned that his task would be a most difficult one, he was told to "open thy mouth, and eat that which I

109

give thee." From this point on let us allow the prophet to tell his own story. He says:

And when I looked, behold a hand was put forth unto me; and, lo, a roll of a book was therein; and he spread it before me: and it was written within and without; and there were written therein lamentations, and mourning, and woe. And he said unto me, Son of man, eat that which thou findest; eat this roll, and go, speak unto the house of Israel. So I opened my mouth and he caused me to eat the roll. And he said unto me, Son of man, cause thy belly to eat, and fill thy bowels with this roll that I give thee. Then did I eat it; and it was in my mouth as honey for sweetness (Ezekiel 2:9 to 3:3).

It was after this experience that Ezekiel was commanded to "get thee unto the house of Israel, and speak with my words unto them." By the symbolism of the eating of the roll, he indicates the necessity of assimilating his message, of making his message a part of himself, as prerequisite to its delivery. He was told, "Fill thy bowels with this roll that I give thee." The message was to become so much a part of the man that it would be impossible to separate the prophet from his prophecy.

John sees himself very much in the position of Ezekiel. He faces a most difficult task in awakening the Christian communities to the seriousness of the impending crisis and of providing the faithful with the encouragement needed by them in the trial of their faith. Under the inspiration of the Spirit, he has arrived now at the realization that he, like Ezekiel, must take his message to himself, heart, mind, and soul.

There is doubtless another parallel in the experiences of the two prophets, and that is the sense of frustration that each feels in respect to his ministry to his own people. Ezekiel was warned that the children of Israel were "impudent and stiffhearted" and that "the house of Israel will not hearken unto thee; for they will not hearken unto me: for all the house of Israel are of a hard forehead and of a stiff heart" (Ezekiel 2:4; 3:7). John was a Jew; he loved his people and he longed

110

for their salvation. But he saw them drifting ever further from acceptance of the gospel. Like Paul, he is forced to consider the relation of Judaism to Christianity; like Paul, he is called upon to interpret Christianity as the fulfilment of the Law and the Prophets, in effect pronouncing the termination of God's dealing with the Hebrews as his chosen people. It is this problem of the relation of Christianity to Judaism that now presents itself to the mind of John as he describes the commission to "measure the temple of God" and the accompanying circumstances of chapter 11. It is an unpleasant task that he faces, but, like Ezekiel, he "makes his face hard" and sets himself to the true prophet's task of speaking the truth.

There is this difference between John's experience and the experience of Ezekiel: while the roll is sweet to his taste as he eats it, his belly was made bitter by the eating. This is a figurative way of saying that the message which, when first received, seemed like honey in the mouth became a cause of apprehension when its demands were made known. It was a message of the uncompromising sovereignty of God in Jesus Christ. This would be a most difficult message to interpret to the "peoples and nations and tongues and kings" concerning whom the prophet is now commanded to prophesy. And it would be equally difficult to apply to his own people, the Jews. But John now moves with the prophetic spirit of Ezekiel of old, and, like the prophet who was sent to "a rebellious house," he arises to discharge his task.

Scene Six

THE MEASURING OF THE TEMPLE, THE TWO PROPHETS, AND THE GREAT EARTHQUAKE

(Chapter 11:1–14)

THE prophet will now deal with the problem of the relation of Israel to the gospel. The vision which began with the appearance of the strong angel holding the little book in his hand continues. The prophet is commanded to "rise, and measure the temple of God, and the altar, and them that worship therein," using the "reed like unto a rod" which had been given him. He is instructed further, "And the court which is without the temple leave without, and measure it not; for it hath been given unto the nations."

The temple of the vision is not in heaven but upon the earth. Apparently the author has in mind the Temple at Jerusalem, for it has a court "without" which had been "given unto the nations." His symbolism is most certainly reminiscent of the court of the Gentiles, which was a part of the Temple area. This Temple, which was built by Herod, had been in ruins twenty-five years when John wrote. But it remained as the symbol of Judaism and all that Judaism stood for. Its destruction had left a question in many minds as to the future of the Jewish state. The most likely explanation of the difficult symbolism of this section is that it is to be understood against the background of the destruction of Jerusalem and the Temple.

What is the meaning of the measuring of the Temple and

112

the command to the prophet that he is not to measure the court of the Gentiles? Does the Temple not represent Judaism, and is not the symbolism designed to suggest that the author is now called upon to make an appraisal of Judaism in the light of the eating of the little book and the demands of the message it contains? Such an interpretation seems to present the fewest difficulties. The outer court of the Temple is representative of the Gentiles—not Christian Gentiles, however. By way of contrast, this court is not to be measured, because no appraisal is to be made of the Gentiles.

The Seer hears that the Holy City will be trodden under foot "forty and two months." The "Holy City" is Jerusalem, and the symbolism is an echo of the destruction of the city by the army of Titus in A.D. 70. The "forty and two months" are three and one-half years, or one-half of the number seven. This is the same length of time that the two witnesses who are called "my two witnesses" prophesy, "clothed in sackcloth." The "forty and two months" and the "thousand two hundred and threescore days" represent short, incomplete periods of time. The two witnesses are more clearly defined by the description in verse six, where it said, "These have the power to shut the heaven, that it rain not during the days of their prophecy: and they have power over the waters to turn them into blood, and to smite the earth with every plague." It was Elijah who had the power to "shut the heaven," and it was Moses who had the "power over the waters to turn them into blood." Elijah was representative of the Prophets, and Moses of the Law in the old dispensation. Both of these prophets appeared on the mount with Jesus in the transfiguration experience. We conclude that the "two witnesses" here stand for the Law and the Prophets. The picture is of these two "clothed in sackcloth" while Jerusalem is destroyed but continuing to prophesy. They are immune to harm while the siege is in progress. It is said, "And if any man desireth to hurt them, fire proceedeth out of their mouth and devoureth their enemies; and if any man shall desire to hurt them, in this manner must he be killed." But they

113

are slain by the "beast that cometh up out of the abyss"; that is, by the emperor or a representative of the imperial Roman power. The conquering general at the capture of Jerusalem was Titus, who later became emperor. With the destruction of the city and the Temple, the author seems to say, the Law and the Prophets appear to lie dead. For "three days and a half" the bodies of the two witnesses lie "in the street of the great city, which spiritually is called Sodom and Egypt, where also their Lord was crucified."

The city is clearly Jerusalem. The author could not have been more pointed in his identification; it is the city where "their Lord was crucified." But he reveals his low estimate of the city by his reference to it as "Sodom" and "Egypt," the former being an outstanding example of wickedness, the latter the standing symbol of Israel's bondage. While thus placing a low appraisal upon the old Jerusalem, he reveals an ardent faith in the enduring qualities of the Law and the Prophets. Notwithstanding the indignities perpetrated upon the bodies of the two witnesses, and despite the fact that the people of the earth made merry over their death, "the breath of life from God entered into them" after the short, inconclusive period of three and a half days (one-half of seven), "and they stood upon their feet." Hearing a voice commanding them to come up to heaven, the two witnesses "went up into heaven in the cloud; and their enemies beheld them." The catastrophe that befell Jerusalem with its dire results are further emphasized in the author's words bringing this vision to its close: "And in that hour there was a great earthquake, and the tenth part of the city fell; and there were killed in the earthquake seven thousand persons: and the rest were affrighted, and gave glory to the God of heaven."

Apparently the author has used the destruction of Jerusalem and the Temple as a background of the imagery here to work out his philosophy of the relation of the gospel to Judaism. He seems to say that the old economy of the theocracy is gone; there is no further place or need for the old

114

Jerusalem. But this does not apply to the Law and the Prophets. It was impossible for these to be destroyed by the evil world power which laid Jerusalem and the Temple low. They were revived with the "breath of life from God" and were "caught up to heaven," by which it is meant that they live and cannot be destroyed. The implication is that they sustain to Christ and to the gospel a relationship which preserves them. If this be John's teaching, he is in his own way repeating the teaching of Jesus. The teaching of Jesus was: "Think not that I came to destroy the law or the prophets: I came not to destroy, but to fulfil. For verily I say unto you, Till heaven and earth pass away, one jot or one tittle shall in no wise pass away from the law, till all things be accomplished" (Matthew 5:17–18). The economy of the kingdom of God preserves that which is eternal in the economy of Israel.

That the Law and the Prophets lived on in the gospel would be a none-too-welcome message to pagans and to certain heretical groups in the Christian communities. The Law and the Prophets had been living witnesses to the holiness of God wherever there was a synagogue. These witnesses had served as a standing judgment against the wickedness and idolatry of the pagans among whom the Jews lived. At this time there was beginning to appear within Christianity anti-Jewish tendencies; and among the Gnostics and Nicolaitans there were those who flouted law and ethics. These were antinomian in practice. A doctrine that the gospel preserved the Law and the Prophets would not be popular among these heretics nor among Christians prejudiced against Jews. On the other hand, the idea that the Jewish economy was done for and that the day of the earthly Jerusalem was over would meet with violent opposition from non-Christian Jews. Thus it will be seen that John had arrived at a conclusion respecting the relation of the gospel to Judaism that would make his message unpopular with many people. It can be seen that his vision of having the roll which he ate make his belly bitter had pointed significance. He could well afford to liken him-

115

self to Ezekiel, who was called to preach to "impudent and stiffhearted" people. We do not wonder that he felt it necessary to eat the book that was in the hand of the angel. The assimilation of the message and dedication to its high demands were essential to its courageous proclamation.

Scene Seven

THE SOUNDING OF THE SEVENTH TRUMPET: PROCLAMATION OF GOD'S SOVEREIGNTY OVER THE WORLD

(Chapter 11:15–19)

THE great proclamation toward which the action of the drama has been moving steadily is now to be made; the stage is set for the sounding of the seventh trumpet. The vision, which is so pregnant with meaning and so vastly important for an understanding of the author's message, is briefly described. When the blast of the trumpet is heard, there are voices in heaven which say,

The kingdom of the world is become *the kingdom* of our Lord, and of his Christ: and he shall reign for ever and ever.

The words italicized, *the kingdom,* do not occur in the original and should be omitted. The translation which appears in the Authorized or King James Version is to be corrected by the better manuscripts and a more faithful rendering of the Greek text. The proclamation appears in the Authorized Version as follows: "The kingdoms of this world are become *the kingdoms* of our Lord, and of his Christ; and he shall reign for ever and ever." The pluralizing of "kingdom" into "kingdoms" indicates a lack of understanding on the part of later scribes of the meaning of the Greek word *basileia.* The scribes, who found the word in the singular and made a plural of it, revealed a misconception that has plagued the minds of many others in framing a concept of the term.

117

MEANING AND MESSAGE OF REVELATION

The English word "kingdom" conveys the idea of territory or of a political entity. It is unfortunate that this connotation of the word has dominated the efforts of those who have sought to interpret the meaning of "kingdom" and of the kingdom of God in the New Testament. It is true that the Greek term *basileia* also has the connotation of "territory" and that it may mean a political entity ruled by a king. But there is another meaning that the Greek word has, and that meaning is "sovereignty" or "rule." Unfortunately the English word "kingdom" does not carry over this meaning, hence it is incapable of correctly representing the idea that is most prominent in the word in its use in the New Testament. That this idea of sovereignty or rule (and it may be added "dominion") is the most common meaning of the word in the New Testament, is plainly evident to any person who will take the trouble to study its usage. It will be found that this is the meaning of the word when it is used so frequently by Jesus in the terms "kingdom of God" and "kingdom of heaven." The kingdom of God is the *rule* or the *dominion* of God. And here in the great proclamation that is revealed when the seventh angel sounds his trumpet, the meaning of the word is most certainly *sovereignty* or *rule.* "The kingdom of the world" means "the rule or sovereignty over the world."

Another point arises in connection with the proper translation of the great proclamation. How shall we translate the verb *egeneto*, which in English is rendered "is become"? It is the aorist indicative of the verb *ginomai*, which means "to become." Normally the aorist is translated "became." The translation "is become," although an English perfect, is allowable in this context. The question as to whether the action is conceived of as having taken place in the past or as a future action that is conceived of as already having taken place in a projected series of events cannot be decided on the basis of the Greek tense. If the latter is the case, the verb would be interpreted in the manner of the Hebrew prophetic perfect; that is, as representing that which is to take place as having already taken place. Whether this is the manner in which the action is to be interpreted must be determined upon the basis of the author's purpose and the entire context of the book. This problem will be discussed presently. At this point we pause to give a proper translation of the great proclamation,

The rule over the world became our Lord's, and his Christ's: and he shall reign for ever and ever.

Taking the proclamation as it reads here, let us inquire as to what it affirms. Clearly it states that, at some point in time, sovereignty over the world became the possession of God and Christ. It should be observed that such a statement does not rule out the fact that God alone exercised at one time sovereignty over the world. The proclamation affirms that the sovereignty over the world came to God and *his Christ*. This is a joint sovereignty of God and Christ which is affirmed here. It is the rule of God in history through his vicegerent, the Messiah, the Anointed One. "And he shall reign for ever and ever" is a reference to the everlasting reign of the Messiah—"he" referring to Christ, though of course God reigns through Christ.

The all-important question that must be answered in the interpretation of the great proclamation is, When in the mind of the author does the sovereignty of God in Christ over the world become a reality? Is this a prediction of the rule of Christ which will become effective with the second advent and the end of the age? This is the interpretation commonly given to the words by most interpreters. If this interpretation be accepted, it affects the interpretation of the book throughout; if it is correct, we shall be compelled to admit that the author's outlook is almost exclusively eschatological and that many other of his visions must be viewed as predictions of the "last days." But it should be borne in mind by those interpreters who would take this reference to the rule of God in Christ as a prophecy of the "last days" that it is impossible to take the words as an expression of the *author's* belief that the end was in the far distant future viewed from his point in history. If this is a prophecy pertaining to the last days, then

119

it must be concluded that the end of the age was near at hand in the author's opinion, for the statement is too closely interwoven with the visions that pertain to things "which must shortly come to pass" to disentangle it from them. It is certain, for instance, that the author was thinking of the sovereignty of God in Christ as opposed to the pretended sovereignty of the Caesars. The beast which represents the imperial rule in chapter 13 is doomed by the lordship and rule of Christ. Are we to believe that the author foresaw the doom of the beast only by the second advent of Christ and the establishment of his reign upon the earth? Is the establishment of the sovereignty of Christ an eschatological victory? These questions cannot be answered apart from an answer to the meaning of the reign of Christ in 11:15. If the reign of Christ in 11:15 is an eschatological reign, then his victory over the beast is an eschatological victory. But the author saw the victory over the beast as taking place in the immediate future. Hence, by this reasoning we must conclude that if the reign of Christ in 11:15 is an eschatological reign, the author foresaw this reign as being established in his own generation. By this reasoning the prophet of the Revelation is made a Seer who erred considerably in his prediction. At the same time doubt is cast upon the value of his whole work, for he is made to be an apocalyptist who not only misjudged the hand of God in history but whose interpretation of history and the gospel is badly weakened by its superficial application to the problems of life.

There is actually but one circumstance that weighs on the side of giving an eschatological interpretation to the great proclamation in 11:15. This is found in the words of the four and twenty elders following the proclamation which have to do with the judgment of the dead and the reward of the servants of God and the saints. The words of the elders are:

> We give thanks, O Lord God, the Almighty, who art and who wast; because thou hast taken thy great power and didst reign. And the nations were wroth, and thy wrath came, and the time of the dead to be judged, and *the time* to give their

120

reward to thy servants the prophets, and to the saints, and to them that fear thy name, the small and the great; and to destroy them that destroy the earth.

The proclamation of the reign of God in Christ is seen to be, by the words of the elders, a time for the dead to be judged and for the reward to be given to God's servants and saints. The reference to the wrath of God here is similar to the mention of the "wrath of the Lamb" in connection with the breaking of the sixth seal (6:16 f.), and it will be recalled that the vision under the opening of the sixth seal was interpreted as a representation of the end of the age. It must be admitted that there are similarities in the description of the judgment described in these two passages. Also, it must be admitted that the reference to the reward of the servants and saints of God in 11:18 is suggestive of the reward to be bestowed upon the righteous at the final judgment. However, the great proclamation of the sovereignty of God in Christ cannot be given an eschatological interpretation solely upon the basis of these considerations; there are matters that weigh heavily upon the other side of the question.

Evidence that *basileia* or reign as exercised by God in Christ need not be referred exclusively to an eschatological reign is found in 12:10, in the words, "a great voice in heaven," which follow the casting down of Satan from heaven. Now the casting down of Satan from heaven follows immediately upon the birth of the Messiah and his catching "up unto God, and unto his throne." This birth of the man Child in chapter 12 can by no stretch of the imagination be interpreted as an event of the last days. As we shall see, it is an apocalyptic representation of the birth of Christ. Now following the description of the birth of the Messiah and his catching up to heaven and of the ensuing war in heaven and casting down of Satan from heaven, a great voice in heaven is heard, saying, "Now is come the salvation, and the power, and the kingdom of our God, and the authority of his Christ."

"Now is come . . . the kingdom (*basileia*) of our God."

121

Clearly the vision is a representation of the establishment of God's kingdom in Christ with the birth of the Messiah and the completion of his work upon the earth. From this passage, then, we are led to the conclusion that the *basileia* of God in Christ began with the incarnation. If this be the meaning of *kingdom* in 12:10, it is its meaning in 11:15. This being the meaning of *kingdom* in 11:15, the references to judgment and reward in 11:18 may be explained on the basis of this interpretation. With the projection of the sovereignty of God into history in the person of Christ, judgment of sinners began, and the reward of the righteous was made certain. By this view the rule of God in Christ makes of both judgment and reward present realities.

Strengthening the view that the proclamation of 11:15 is an announcement of the reign of God which began with the incarnation, is the fact that the next great vision in order portrays, as we have seen, the birth of Christ. The close proximity of this portrayal of the birth of the Messiah to the great proclamation of God's sovereignty in Christ in 11:15 strongly suggests that in the author's mind the *basileia* and the incarnation were inseparable.

The view that the assertion of the sovereignty of God in 11:15 is a proclamation of his rule in history, beginning with the incarnation, is further strengthened by the Old Testament concept of Messiah's reign and by the interpretation of this concept by the early church. The proclamation in 11:15 is of the reign of God through his Anointed, the Messiah. The statement is no denial of the sovereignty of God over the universe from the beginning of time; it is an affirmation of the projection of that sovereignty into history in the person of his Son, Jesus Christ: "The rule over the world became our Lord's and his Christ's." The proclamation, together with the accompanying statement in 11:18 that "the nations were wroth," is reminiscent of Psalm 2:1: "Why do the nations rage, and the peoples meditate a vain thing? The kings of the earth set themselves, and the rulers take counsel together, against Jehovah and against his anointed." The words were taken as a messianic prophecy by the members of the Jerusalem church in the early days of Christianity. When Peter and John returned to the group from their imprisonment, the Christian company burst forth into a prayer, which evidently had been memorized as a corporate prayer, and which contains the earliest statement of Christian creed on record. This remarkable liturgical statement, which is found in Acts 4:24–30, begins by the recitation of Psalm 2:1 given above and continues:

> for of a truth in this city against thy holy Servant Jesus, whom thou didst anoint, both Herod and Pontius Pilate, with the Gentiles and the peoples of Israel, were gathered together, to do whatsoever thy hands and thy counsel foreordained to come to pass. And now, Lord, look upon their threatenings: and grant unto thy servants to speak thy word with all boldness, while thou stretchest forth thy hand to heal; and that signs and wonders may be done through the name of thy holy Servant Jesus.

It is clear that these early Christians saw in the crucifixion of Jesus and in the persecution to which they were being subjected the fulfilment of the prophecy of Psalm 2:1. Now this psalm speaks of the kings and the rulers of the earth setting themselves against "Jehovah, and against his anointed." The "anointed" of Jehovah is his *Christ* (in the Greek, *Christos*). The "anointed" of Jehovah is taken to be a reference to the Messiah by the early Christian group, and of course Jesus of Nazareth is for them the Messiah. Clearly they see the rule of God in Christ as a present reality and set in opposition to Herod, Pilate, the Gentiles, and all earthly rule. This consciousness of the early Christians of the present reign of God in Christ is further emphasized in the sermon of Peter at Pentecost. Peter brings his sermon to a conclusion with a ringing declaration of the lordship and reign of Jesus as Messiah. He declares:

> This Jesus did God raise up, whereof we are all witnesses. Being therefore by the right hand of God exalted, and having

received of the Father the promise of the Holy Spirit, he hath poured forth this, which ye see and hear. For David ascended not into the heavens: but he saith himself, The Lord saith unto my Lord, Sit thou on my right hand, till I make thine enemies the footstool of thy feet. Let all the house of Israel therefore know assuredly, that God hath made him both Lord and Christ, this Jesus whom ye crucified (Acts 2:32–36).

Now these passages from Acts clearly establish the fact that in the early Christian community the present reign or kingdom of God in Jesus Christ, the Messiah, was an accepted and vigorously asserted doctrine. It is therefore no new doctrine of the present *basileia* of God in Christ that we meet with in Revelation. The doctrine was as old as the Christian community itself. When the Seer of Patmos declares that "the kingdom over the world became our Lord's and his Christ's," he is reasserting, in the face of the claims of the "kings of the earth," to be divine the doctrine that the primitive Christian community had enunciated when it faced persecution at the hands of the "rulers of the people."

The great proclamation in 11:15 is also to be interpreted in the light of the great passage in Daniel 7:13–14, a passage which was interpreted messianically in the early Christian communities. Whatever may have been the intent of the author of this passage as to the meaning of the term "son of man," the term was understood in the first century as referring to an individual. Jesus used the term as a designation of himself as Messiah. In this passage, therefore, in the minds of Jesus and the early Christian teachers, there is pictured the everlasting dominion to be bestowed upon the Messiah. The passage is as follows:

I saw in the night-visions, and, behold, there came with the clouds of heaven one like unto a son of man, and he came even to the ancient of days, and they brought him near before him. And there was given him dominion, and glory, and a kingdom, that all the peoples, nations, and languages should

124

serve him: his dominion is an everlasting dominion, which shall not pass away, and his kingdom that which shall not be destroyed.

The Gospels, which were written before Revelation was written, present Jesus as the Son of man. This is proof that the term was current in the Christian communities before Revelation came into existence. The concept of the Son of man in the Christian communities was in keeping with this concept we find in Daniel, and here it is of the Son of man who receives from God (the "ancient of days") an everlasting kingdom. Taken with the interpretation of Messiah's present reign which we find in Acts, we may be certain that the everlasting dominion of the Son of man met with in Daniel was likewise conceived of as a dominion which began with the exaltation of Christ to the right hand of God.

In the light of this clearly defined tradition in the early church that Christ had received from God the everlasting dominion, we may conclude that, in his proclamation of the sovereignty of God in Christ which would last "for ever and ever," John was affirming the great eternal reign of God in Christ that then existed and that began with the incarnation of God in Christ.

What practical aim does the author have in reasserting this great doctrine of early Christian faith? It is to assure the Christian communities that there is no king but Christ, in spite of the claims of the Caesars to be divine. It is to warn lukewarm Christians that Christ will tolerate no allegiance to any other sovereignty than his own sovereignty over the lives of God's people. It is to encourage the persecuted Christian communities to believe that in Christ God retains the controls of history and will work out the divine purpose in history. If God was sovereign before the incarnation, as indeed he was, he has now by a mighty act entered history, with the result that his sovereign rule is comprehensible and realizable on the basis of the revelation of his will in the life and the work of the man Jesus. It is true that this rule of God in Christ assures no perfect society among men. It is true that evil rulers and the multitudes of sinners still set themselves against the rule of God, but a perfect order in society in which there is no sin and no evil men is not contemplated by the sovereignty of God in Christ. The New Testament teaches the existence of no perfect society in history; the existence of the perfect order is reserved for the dispensation beyond history. But the reign of God in history does contemplate a good society in which the revelation of truth in Christ is regnant; it does contemplate a society in which Satan is not regnant and in which sin is conquered. Likewise the sovereign reign of God in Christ assures the ongoing in the world and the progressive acceptance by humanity of the truth of God in Christ. Under the sovereign reign of God, men assert and live by this truth; and they validate this truth in the demonstration of its value; thus do they pass it on to other generations. The present reign of God in Christ, though that reign is far from being accepted by all men, is a pledge that God will reign perfectly beyond history. Thus in this kingdom the hope of the life everlasting and its rewards are kept alive in the hearts of men. By this hope they are inspired to give unstintedly of their devotion to Christ's cause and to stake all upon the belief that his way is "the way, and the truth, and the life." In this assurance men accept suffering and death with resignation and courage, knowing that God worketh "all things together for good to them that love him."

The Seer of Patmos has reasserted the great doctrine of the Christian faith that Christ is King of kings and Lord of lords. From this point on his book will reveal the dramatic challenge to this sovereignty by an earthly sovereignty inspired by Satan. As his book draws to its close, we shall see the issue of this challenge in the vindication of his sublime assurance that Christ is King and that he shall reign for ever and ever.

ACT TWO

The Conflict of Sovereignties and the Victory of God: Messiah's Birth and Victory over Satan, the New Heaven and the New Earth, and the New Jerusalem.—12:1 to 22:5.

✝

Scene One

MESSIAH'S BIRTH AND ESCAPE FROM THE DRAGON SATAN, THE FALL OF SATAN AND HIS ANGELS, THE PERSECUTION OF THE WOMAN AND HER SEED

(Chapter 12)

GOD'S sovereignty over the world in Jesus Christ has been proclaimed. By the series of visions under the breaking of the seals of the scroll, John has shown how that sovereignty stands as an established fact over against the problems of history which seem to deny it. But now it remains to portray the manner in which this rule of God has been projected into history and how its projection precipitates the inevitable conflict with the Caesars. The story of Revelation from this point on is the story of the conflict between the sovereignty of God in Jesus Christ and the pretended sovereignty of Satan expressed through the rulers of Rome. The issue of this conflict, its implications for the churches, and its outcome are to be traced in dramatic apocalyptic fashion. The grand victory of Christ over his enemies on the plane of history will be illustrated in vivid symbols. Beyond the victory of Christ in history, the Seer of Patmos will peer into the mysteries of the world to come to paint an incomparable picture of the new heaven and the new earth and the grand final victory of the people of God in the new Jerusalem.

Act Two, the new movement of the great drama, takes its

rise in heaven. In this it is similar to Act One, which began with the vision of the Sovereign of the universe seated upon the throne in the Court of Heaven. The opening vision is of "a woman arrayed with the sun, and the moon under her feet, and upon her head a crown of twelve stars; and she was with child; and she crieth out, travailing in birth, and in pain to be delivered."

The author is preparing to give in apocalyptic fashion an account of the birth of Christ. His imagery can be interpreted in no other satisfactory way. The statement of verse 5 is the undeniable clue to this. This verse states that the woman "was delivered of a son, a man child, who is to rule all the nations with a rod of iron." The child who "is to rule all the nations with a rod of iron" is clearly identified as the Anointed of Jehovah whose reign is described in Psalm 2. A passage of the psalm reads: "Jehovah said unto me, Thou art my son; this day have I begotten thee. Ask of me, and I will give *thee* the nations for thine inheritance, And the uttermost parts of the earth for thy possession. Thou shalt break them with a rod of iron; Thou shalt dash them in pieces like a potter's vessel." The psalm was interpreted by the early Christian community, as has been seen, as a messianic psalm, describing the reign of the Christ. We have observed in the study of the great proclamation of 11:15 how it was the background, along with Daniel 7:13–14, of this assertion of the sovereignty of God in Christ and the everlasting reign of the Messiah. Clearly now the author is describing the birth of Jehovah's Anointed and the beginning of Messiah's everlasting reign.

The woman represents Israel, or that portion of Israel from which Messiah was born. Later in the account, as she is persecuted by the dragon, apparently she becomes the Christian community. Charles points out in a long discussion of the identity of the woman that there are many close parallels in the Old Testament in which the theocratic community is described as a woman in travail, as Isaiah 26:17; Micah 4:10; and Isaiah 66:7. He says: "The above passages, which compare the theocratic community in travail (cf. also Jer. iv. 31, xiii. 21, xxii. 23; Isa. xiii. 8, xxi. 3; Hos. xiii. 13), and the birth of the new Israel to that of a man child (Isa. lxvi. 7 sq.), point to the fact that this vision in its Jewish form dealt with the expected birth of the Messiah from the Jewish nation, and that in its present and Christian context it refers to the birth of Christ."[1] In Galatians 4:26, Paul refers to "the Jerusalem that is above" as "our mother." Here the "mother" represents the ideal people of God, Jewish and Gentile Christians alike. There is precedent, therefore, for John's use of the figure of the woman to represent Israel and the people of God.

In the vision a great red dragon appears prepared to devour the child as soon as it is born. The dragon is identified in verse 9 as "the old serpent, he that is called the Devil and Satan, the deceiver of the whole world." The "seven heads and ten horns" of the dragon and the "seven diadems" upon his head represent his great authority and power. His great control over earthly and heavenly powers and his sinister influence over the rulers of earth can be seen from the statement, "And his tail draweth the third part of the stars of heaven, and did cast them to the earth."

This strange imagery of the dragon, crouched and ready to destroy the Child when it is born, is a vivid portrayal of the initiation of the great conflict between God and Satan in history. This attempt of Satan to destroy the Messiah from the very beginning emphasizes the deadly and uncompromising nature of the conflict from its inception. Satan is portrayed as being fully cognizant of the implications of the great birth about to take place. He recognizes the fact that with the coming of God in the flesh great forces will be set in motion which are certain to result in great reductions of his power. He sees that a ceaseless struggle for the preservation of that power now looms. Perhaps John has in the background of his thinking the actual effort of an evil world ruler, Herod, to destroy the Messiah when he is born. The unsuccessful effort of that Satan-inspired ruler to destroy the Messiah was

[1]*The Revelation of St. John,* Vol. I, p. 317.

repeated in the crucifixion of Christ when the Roman Government conspired with the Jewish officials to put Jesus to death. These historical facts are doubtless the inspiration in part of these symbolic representations. The efforts of Satan through these rulers to destroy the Messiah failed. In the vision John describes this historical fact in these words: "And the child was caught up unto God, and unto his throne." This may well be a representation of the account of the ascension of Christ.

Upon the rescue of her Child from the wrath of the dragon, "the woman fled into the wilderness, where she hath a place prepared of God, that there they may nourish her a thousand two hundred and threescore days." This enigmatic symbol of time is to be equated with "a time, and times, and half a time" in 12:14. It is the same length of time that the two witnesses of 11:3 prophesy. It symbolizes a period of persecution that is limited in duration. The "time, and times, and half a time" is meant to suggest three and a half years. The "thousand two hundred and threescore days" are roughly three and a half years. This persecution of the woman is reminiscent of the persecution of the early Jewish-Christian community. The second account of the persecution of the woman after the casting down of Satan from heaven may well refer to the experience of the Christian community in its flight from Jerusalem to Pella in connection with the siege that led up to the capture of the city by Titus in A.D. 70. John says, "And there were given to the woman the two wings of the great eagle, that she might fly into the wilderness unto her place, where she is nourished for a time, and times, and half a time, from the face of the serpent."

The rescue of the man Child from the serpent precipitates a continuation of the great conflict in heaven: "And there was war in heaven: Michael and his angels *going forth* to war with the dragon; and the dragon warred and his angels; and they prevailed not, neither was their place found any more in heaven. And the great dragon was cast down, the old serpent, he that is called the Devil and Satan, the deceiver of the whole world; he was cast down to the earth, and his angels were cast down with him."

The mighty act of God in bringing to birth the Messiah is the great and final challenge to the dominion of Satan. The conflict that is set in motion does not involve earth alone; it is cosmic in its extent, because the incarnation is a cosmic event. John has portrayed in apocalyptic imagery the supernatural and heavenly aspects of the vast warfare. The warfare must be fought out in heaven as well as upon the earth. Satan is defeated in the heavenly battle; he and his angels are cast down to earth. In this fashion is symbolized the great defeat suffered by Satan in the birth of Jesus and in his establishment as Messiah. This was indeed Satan's sorest defeat. This fall of Satan was recognized by Jesus during his earthly ministry; and there is an echo of his words in this representation of his defeat in the Revelation. When the seventy returned from the mission tour upon which they had been sent by Jesus and reported to him that even the demons had been subject to them, Jesus exclaimed in exultation, "I beheld Satan fall [correct rendering of the Greek aorist participle] as lightning from heaven" (Luke 10:18). The defeat of the demons was a defeat of Satan at the hands of Christ. Jesus recognized the cosmic nature of this great defeat in describing it in much the same terms as we have it described in Revelation: it was a fall of Satan from heaven.

But the casting down of Satan from heaven by no means effects his destruction. His appearance upon the earthly scene is the signal for the continuation of the struggle in the world and in history. A vast cosmic victory has been won with the establishment of Jesus of Nazareth as the Messiah, but a deadly warfare is now to begin in the world. Satan will incarnate himself in evil world rulers, even as God has incarnated himself in his Son Jesus Christ, and through these evil men of flesh and blood he will seek to defeat the purposes of God in history. This is the background of the struggle that is to be carried forward from the thirteenth chapter almost to the end; it explains the rise of the beasts and their warfare.

These we shall observe at close range presently, but let us pause here to see what the state of affairs will be with the children of God as they are caught in this violent conflict. John gives a foregleam of their victory in these significant words:

> Now is come the salvation, and the power, and the kingdom of our God, and the authority of his Christ: for the accuser of our brethren is cast down, who accuseth them before our God day and night. And they overcame him because of the blood of the Lamb, and because of the word of their testimony; and they loved not their life even unto death. Therefore rejoice, O heavens, and ye that dwell in them. Woe for the earth and for the sea; because the devil is gone down unto you, having great wrath, knowing that he hath but a short time.

With the birth of Christ and his firm establishment, in spite of his crucifixion as King-Messiah, the *salvation* and the *power* and the *kingdom* of God, and the *authority of his Christ* are all realities, fruits of the casting down of Satan from heaven. Thus the salvation of God's people is an accomplished fact. The great deed of God's entry into humanity has been done; no power in heaven or on earth can retrieve that deed. Christ has come off victorious from the great struggle and is now established as King of kings and Lord of lords. God will not retreat; he cannot retreat from the great entry he has made through Christ into the affairs of men for their redemption. God has answered the great Accuser of men by clothing himself with human flesh for their salvation. And now there is provided for all the children of God a means of victory over the great Accuser as he proceeds to bring woe upon the earth. The great Accuser has "but a short time"; that is, his days· of activity among men are few in number as days are counted in the eternal scheme of things. Indeed, the "last age" of human history has begun, because God's final act for man's salvation has been accomplished. With the completion of these "last days," Satan's career will come to its end. But meanwhile he will "go up and down upon the earth like a roaring lion seeking whom he may destroy." And how shall the people of God withstand him? "And they overcame him because of the blood of the Lamb, and because of the word of their testimony; and they loved not their life even unto death."

The prophet sees the victory of God's people upon the earth as already won because of the victory Christ has won over Satan: "They *overcame* him" is his way of voicing his confidence in their certain victory. Here in these few words is the formula for Christian victory in the struggle of this earthly existence. The source and power of our victory are the *blood of the Lamb*. This is God's part in salvation. The sacrificial death of Christ is that aspect of salvation in which man has no part; it is a deed that is done; it is of God; no merit in man and no good deeds on his part can contribute to or affect this great thing that God has done for man's redemption. But man identifies himself with God's great act of redemption in Christ, by faith, and his victory over Satan is assured, because Christ's victory becomes his victory. But the victory is continued in the believer's obedience to God. This obedience is demonstrated (1) in the word of his testimony, and (2) in the fact that he loves not his life even unto death. "The word of their testimony"—what is it? It is the living witness that we give in word, life, and deed to the gospel. This is the word of truth in Jesus Christ; it is testimony to Jesus Christ and his power to save; it is witness to his teachings and his wonderful life among men; it is the testimony concerning him given by those who know him through experience. And who are those who love not their life unto death? They are those followers of Jesus Christ who have taken seriously his Word, "He that loseth his life for my sake shall find it"; they are those who, like Christ, are willing to seal their witness with their blood; they are those who hold not their lives dear in the fight for righteousness and justice upon the earth; they are the children of the Kingdom whom the love of power and of the world cannot corrupt.

Armed with the power of the blood of the Lamb and with

these weapons of testimony and complete self-giving, Christ's people upon the earth are assured of victory in life and death over the great Adversary of their souls and Accuser of their brethren.

As the dragon goes forth to make war with the woman's seed, those who have been redeemed in the blood of the Lamb are armed for the conflict.

```
*************************
*                       *
*      Scene Two        *
*                       *
*************************
```

SATAN CONTINUES HIS WARFARE AGAINST
CHRIST THROUGH TWO BEASTS

(Chapter 13)

BY the victory of Christ over Satan in his exaltation to the
right hand of God after his redemptive work on earth,
the issue has been joined between the two within the
framework of history. John in his visions now brings the
cosmic drama to earth and reveals its unfolding among men
and in events of his own time. Specifically he deals with the
problem of emperor worship as this problem touches the
lives of the churches and Christian believers. The demand of
the emperor that he be paid divine honors was no light matter; it involved the loyalty of the individual to the lordship of
Christ and the whole Christian concept of man's obligation
to the invisible God. It threatened to destroy the foundations
of the Christian concept of society, for those foundations
were built largely upon the freedom of the individual to
worship God and upon the ethical ideals transmitted to the
Christian communities by Jesus Christ. The Seer of Patmos
saw that the issue was much larger than the obeisance of
an individual to the statue of the emperor; he recognized that
other evils stemmed from this initial surrender to an earthly
sovereign who made the blasphemous claim to be divine. One
of these was the price of total surrender of the life that the
individual paid to Satan and the Caesar in bowing to a man
as a god. John saw that, once the individual surrenders
religious liberty, he surrenders to a totalitarianism that leaves

137

him with no freedom of action and no will of his own. Once he gives spiritual allegiance to an earthly ruler or government, the giving of lesser loyalties can be expected. Under a totalitarian concept such as emperor worship fostered, church and state were merged, so that a religious institution became an arm of the state to enforce the will of the state upon all. The political, cultural, and economic life of the people was encompassed in such a scheme. The officials and priests of the cult of emperor worship became the inquisitors who were zealous to enforce the emperor's wishes that he be paid divine honors; they were eager also to bring to the bar of Roman law courts those who dared defy the order to make a sacrifice before the emperor's statue.

The crisis that confronted the churches was made more serious by the element of patriotism involved in the tradition of emperor worship. Rome had achieved great success in unifying the Mediterranean world and in bringing into one vast political organization many diverse nationalities and political units. The empire had brought peace and order and a measure of prosperity to a good portion of the civilized world. She fostered a measure of freedom and self-government among subjugated peoples. It was an honor to be a Roman citizen. The emperor had become the symbol of this vast unifying force. It was a mark of patriotism to do him honor. With the masses it was no cause for alarm that the emperors from time to time had asserted a claim to be descended from the gods. Doubtless many of the more educated members of the population put no faith in the truth of the claim, but they accepted the custom as a wholesome aid to patriotism and cheerfully entered into the performance of those rites demanded by it. At the same time they would look with quick suspicion upon those individuals who saw anything wrong with the custom or refused to perform the necessary rites. Such an attitude on the part of the many would make the lot of the Christians harder in those communities where emperor worship was made an issue.

The unity of the political and religious forces of the empire, together with the easy acceptance by the masses of emperor worship as a rallying principle of patriotism, would readily prepare the way for the designation by Christians of the empire as the empire of Satan in the issue that arose between the Caesars and Christianity. The Christian group, in its refusal to compromise with emperor worship, found itself arrayed against the empire and not simply against the emperor and the provincial authorities. John had no difficulty, therefore, in thinking of the empire as ruled by Satan and in designating the emperor and the priests of the emperor cult as beasts working under the direction of Satan.

The First Beast Is Given Authority by the Dragon to Persecute the Saints.—13:1-10

The vision that now comes to John is of a beast that came up out of the sea as the Seer stood upon the shore of the sea. (The correct reading here is, "And I stood upon the sand of the sea.") The ten horns which this beast possesses are symbols of his great power. He has seven heads, these representing the succession of emperors, or the imperial Roman power. The ten diadems he wears are symbols of his authority. The beast has "names of blasphemy" written upon his head. These are suggestive of the names used by the emperors in their efforts to encourage the belief that they were divine. One of these was *augustus* (Octavius, the first of the emperors, took this title). Another of these names was *theos*, the Greek word for God. Still another was *kyrios*, "lord"; and yet another was *sotēr*, "savior."

The beast is Satan's representative. This is seen from the statement, "The dragon gave him his power, and his throne, and great authority." John continues, "And I *saw* one of his heads as though it had been smitten unto death; and his deathstroke was healed." The most reasonable explanation of this head with the deathstroke that had been healed is that it reflects the Nero-*redivivus* myth. According to this myth, Nero was to come back to life, perhaps at the head of an army

139

from Parthia, and re-establish himself as emperor. Of course John did not believe the myth, but he used it to identify the beast as the Antichrist. Nero had been the vilest and most wicked of the emperors. He had burned the city of Rome and laid the crime to the charge of the Christians who suffered martyrdom in great numbers at his hands. His record was well known to the Christian communities all over the empire. By the symbolism here John invests the succession of emperors with the characteristics of Nero, the worst of all the emperors. At the same time he may have intended to suggest that in Domitian, the reigning emperor, Nero had come back alive, and that because of this the churches might expect from him the same sort of treatment the Roman Christians had received from Nero.

The beast receives the worship and acclaim of the multitudes: "And the whole earth wondered after the beast; and they worshipped the dragon, because he gave his authority unto the beast; and they worshipped the beast, saying, Who is like unto the beast? and who is able to war with him?" This is a representation of the popularity of emperor worship throughout the empire and of the ready acceptance by the populace of the demands of the emperor that he be worshiped as a god. The beast was given "a mouth speaking great things and blasphemies; and there was given to him authority to continue forty and two months." Again we meet with the "forty and two months" or three-and-a-half-year period, a figure which is used to designate a limited period of persecution. John continues, "And he opened his mouth for blasphemies against God, to blaspheme his name, and his tabernacle, even them that dwell in the heaven" [Greek, "those tabernacling in heaven"].

Again we are impressed with the fact that John is a realist. He will make no promise that Christians will escape the wrath of the emperor if they fail to worship his statues. He says, "And it was given unto him to make war with the saints, and to overcome them." Furthermore, the emperor will succeed in his purpose to secure universal obedience to his

140

wishes—with the exception only of Christians. "And there was given to him authority over every tribe and people and tongue and nation. And all that dwell on the earth shall worship him, every one whose name hath not been written in the book of life of the Lamb slain from the foundation of the world." (This translation of the final part of this passage is preferred to the translation which reads, "whose name hath not been written from the foundation of the world in the book of life of the Lamb that hath been slain.") By this prophecy is given to us a glimpse of the isolation into which the little Christian communities would likely be forced by their rebellion against the policy of the emperor. Over against the great empire, its emperor, its officials, and its legions, the little groups of Christians would be compelled to stand alone. Their consolation would be their knowledge that, though their names were not enrolled in the lists of citizens of the empire, they were written in the book presided over by the Lamb slain from the foundation of the world. Thus was their redemption secure, for it had its origin in the eternal purposes of God. The author of their salvation was the Lamb who from the beginning was the slain Lamb, since his appearance in time and history was the outgoing of God's eternal plan of redemption. The Caesar might have his little day, but that day would soon be done. Above time and space the Lamb presided in eternity over that book which contained the names of those who had been bought with his precious blood.

The children of God are not to take up arms against the Caesars and seek to defend themselves by force in this struggle. This is the lesson of the warning that now comes from the pen of the Seer. "If any man is for captivity, into captivity he goeth: if any man shall kill with the sword, with the sword must he be killed. Here is the patience and faith of the saints." John seems to mean by these words that the warfare of the saints is spiritual; they are not to seek to defend the gospel or themselves with the sword in their loyalty to the gospel. Captivity only produces captivity for

141

him who seeks to take others captive; he who takes the sword shall die by the sword. To abide by this principle is the patience and the faith of the saints!

The Second Beast Compels Men to Worship the First Beast.—13:11–18

The second beast represents the priests or officials of the cult of emperor worship. The description John gives of this creature leaves little doubt that this is the meaning of his symbolism.

The second beast comes up out of the earth. He has two horns "like unto a lamb, and he spake as a dragon." The horns of the lamb are intended to convey the apparent harmless nature of the beast; but these horns belie the voice of the creature; he speaks as a dragon; that is, with the voice of Satan. His harmless exterior is therefore pretended and hypocritical. He is a false prophet and is so identified in 19:20. In contrast with the true prophet who receives his commission from the living God, this false prophet receives his orders from an earthly ruler. Here is revealed one of the characteristic marks of the false prophet in any age—he is subservient to men and temporal authority. The function of this beast is to secure obedience to the first beast and bring all the people of the empire to worship him. "And he exerciseth all the authority of the first beast in his sight. And he maketh the earth and them that dwell therein to worship the first beast, whose deathstroke was healed." It was the duty of the priests of the emperor cult to promote, with the assistance and supervision of the provincial officials, the worship of the emperor and perform the rites connected with the worship. It is suggested by the imagery that follows that the priests were capable of practicing magic and impressing worshipers with signs which were done during the festivals and ceremonies held before the statue of the emperor. "And he doeth great signs, that he should even make fire to come down out of heaven upon the earth in the sight of men. And

142

he deceiveth them that dwell on the earth by reason of the signs which it was given him to do in the sight of the beast; saying to them that dwell on the earth, that they should make an image of the beast who hath the stroke of the sword and lived." The magic seems even to have extended to the ability of the priests to endow the statue of the emperor with the appearance of life: "And it was given unto him to give breath to it, even to the image of the beast, that the image of the beast should both speak, and cause that as many as should not worship the image of the beast should be killed." Perhaps the art of ventriloquism was used by the priests to give the statue the appearance of speaking. It seems that through such a trick the statue could be made to pronounce the dictum of death for all who would not worship the emperor's statue. Swete says at this point:

> Thus in the immediate view of the Seer the second Beast represents the sorcery and superstition of the age as engaged in a common attempt to impose the Caesar-cult upon the provinces, behind which there lay the Satanic purpose of bringing ruin upon the rising Christian brotherhoods. In its wider significance the symbol may well stand for any religious system which allies itself with the hostile forces of the world against the faith of Jesus Christ.[1]

So great was the power of the priesthood of the emperor cult that it was able to impose social and economic ostracism upon those who refused to participate in emperor worship. At least we may say that John foresaw that the priesthood would have this power as the crisis deepened and the resistance of the Christians grew stronger. This is what is meant by the statement, "And he causeth all, the small and the great, and the rich and the poor, and the free and the bond, that there be given them a mark on their right hand, or upon their forehead; and that no man should be able to buy or to sell, save he that hath the mark, even the name of the beast or the number of his name." It is not necessary to think that

[1] *The Apocalypse of St. John*, p. 172.

not

this suggests that actual marks would be placed upon the loyal worshipers of the Caesar. It is to represent the manner in which those who refused to participate in emperor worship would be ostracized and how that ostracism would affect their economic life. What John is suggesting is that loyal Christians faced a threat to their very physical existence. Loyalty to Christ and refusal to worship the emperor would bring discrimination against the Christian communities that would affect and limit their "buying and selling"; that is, their economic life and their business transactions. The imposition of such ostracism could be secured through the co-operation of the provincial officials and the aid of business enterprises loyal to the emperor. The populace, fired by patriotism and prejudice, would quickly fall in with such discrimination. This type of discrimination, related as it was to religious prejudice and persecution, is not difficult to engender. It has been practiced many times in history. Minority groups have often been the victims of such discrimination. Christians in Europe, Jews in Europe and America, and Negroes in the United States have been the victims of a type of economic ostracism similar to that which threatened the Christian communities in the last years of the first century. In the case of the Christian communities in the first century, the ostracism would be aggravated by the fact that, by their refusal to worship the emperor, the Christians could be charged with disloyalty to the government and lack of patriotism. This element of disloyalty to the state has also entered into persecuting movements of later times. The charge of disloyalty to the government is often connected with the loyalty of groups to their own religious convictions.

This persecution and ostracism in prospect for the Christians of the first century were the outgrowth of a union of state and religion, in which religion became simply an arm of the state and subservient to the temporal power. It is an illustration of what takes place when the state is able to dictate to its citizens the character of their religious faith and practice. It vividly illustrates the evils of a system which unites

144

church and state. Once a people surrenders its religious liberty, it has in effect delivered its life to the state. This is seen in the authority of the priests of the emperor to place the "mark of the beast" on loyal worshipers and to inflict economic ostracism upon the Christians of the first century. This same invasion of the private lives of individuals on the basis of the surrender of their religious liberty was re-enacted in recent years in Germany, where Hitler became a god and nazism a state religion. Hitler became the owner of the lives and souls of his subjects, because he was able to take away their freedom to worship God as their consciences dictated. There were those like Niemoeller who refused to allow Hitler to be the lord of their lives. Many of these suffered martyrdom in their resistance to the demonic Nazi system, but they brought undying glory to the cause of Christ in their rebellion against the blasphemous claims of an earthly ruler who assumed the prerogatives of God.

The evils of the church-state system are the same in any age. Whenever such a system is established, liberty dies for those who must live under it. The advocates of such a system are somewhat vocal today. Lovers of liberty may well look back to the crisis that confronted the church in the last years of the first century and learn from the lessons of the two beasts that so vividly portray the death of freedom under the alliance of a religious institution with the state.

Let us, in conclusion, inquire into the meaning of the "number of the beast." To conclude the description of this scene, John says: "Here is wisdom. He that understandeth, let him count the number of the beast; for it is the number of a man: and his number is Six hundred and sixty and six." Various suggestions have been made for the interpretation of the enigmatical number. One is that by the triplication of the number 6, which is one short of the perfect number 7, John means to suggest the imperfection and inherent weakness of the emperor. This is possible, but a more likely interpretation is that the number is a representation of the name, Nero Caesar. This conclusion is arrived at in this manner: The

145

name *Neron Kaisar* in Greek is transliterated into Hebrew letters, and the Hebrew letters are then given their equivalents in numerals. (The Greeks and the Hebrews did not use the Arabic system of numbers but employed the letters of the alphabet to stand for numbers; for instance, Alpha, the first letter in the Greek alphabet, stood for 1; Aleph, the first letter in the Hebrew alphabet, stood for 1.) Now when *Neron Kaisar* is transliterated into Hebrew characters and the sum total of the Hebrew characters as numerals is taken, the resulting total is 666. The Hebrew letters, as numerals, are as follows: Nun=50; Resh=200; Vav=6; Nun=50—this is *Neron;* Qoph=100; Samech=60; Resh=200—this is *Kaisar.* The numerals added give 666.

John uses such a device to indicate to the Asian Christians that the beast was actually a man, and a man who would have the spirit of the hated Nero. By this designation of the emperor, John would warn the Christians of what they were to expect from the imperial power, and at the same time he would protect them in the possession of a book that at once would identify its possessors as disloyal to the Roman Government. Above all, he would reveal to the Christian communities that they faced the wrath of a ruler who could be designated Antichrist.

SEVEN ASSURANCES AND WARNINGS FOR
THE GREAT CONFLICT

(Chapter 14)

THE description of the beasts in chapter 13 has introduced us to the nature of the great conflict to be precipitated upon the earth. The fierceness of the struggle is indicated by the character of the adversaries now set against the Christian churches. Before proceeding with an account of the conflict, the author pauses for one of the "interludes" which now and again appear to interrupt the action. With the revelation of the impending struggle before him, the author is concerned that his readers shall fully understand the security of the people of God. By way of contrast with their own security, he wishes them to visualize the certain doom of the enemies of God. Underneath his purpose of thus giving assurance to faithful Christians is the added purpose of warning all who would set themselves against God. The warning will serve as a stimulus to lukewarm Christians and at the same time provide a pronouncement of judgment upon the wicked. These warnings and assurances may be analyzed in the following manner:

1. *The redeemed of earth are in close communion with the hosts of heaven (14:1–5).*—This is the lesson we derive from this intriguingly beautiful picture of the redeemed of earth standing with the Lamb on Mount Zion. Again we meet with the one hundred and forty-four thousand. In chapter 7 we identified them as the redeemed of God upon the earth. The

147

identification made in connection with the vision of chapter 7 is justified in the description of the one hundred and forty-four thousand here. They are standing with the Lamb "on the mount Zion . . . having his name, and the name of his Father, written on their foreheads." The sealing which they were described in 7:3 as having received remains in effect. By way of contrast with the worshipers of the Caesar who have received the "mark of the beast," these have the name of God and the Lamb upon them. This is a way of saying that the character of God and of Christ has been communicated to them—they are children of God by reason of the transmission by God to them of his own essence and being in Christ.

The Seer in his vision hears music in heaven. He describes that which comes to the ears of the spirit in words of poetic beauty: "And I heard a voice from heaven, as the voice of many waters, and as the voice of a great thunder: and the voice which I heard was as the voice of harpers harping with their harps." The harmonies which John hears come from a heavenly choir. It is a "new song before the throne, and before the four living creatures and the elders." Now the lesson that the Seer is anxious for those who face persecution to learn is that heaven and its blessings are very near for the people of God. The redeemed of earth in the midst of their tribulation may be *en rapport* with heaven. The line between the temporal and the eternal fades for those who love the Lord. "No man could learn the song save the hundred and forty and four thousand, even they that had been purchased out of the earth." But there is a heavenly song which the redeemed of earth may learn. They qualify by their fidelity to the Lamb and by the holiness of their lives to learn the song. They are clean in their moral lives: they are not "defiled with women" and they are "virgins"; by which is meant they are not contaminated with the sexual vices which were so common among the pagans. These who are capable of learning the heavenly song "follow the Lamb whithersoever he goeth." By this imagery it is meant that the believers who have been truly redeemed obey the command of Jesus, "Follow me!" That is a command which requires the renunciation of all to follow Christ, and the obedience of the disciple to the teachings and example of the Teacher. The Lamb in this vision, it is to be remembered, is upon the earth with his people who stand in solid security on Mount Zion, a symbol of the unshakeable foundation upon which God's people are set. The redeemed in this vision "were purchased from among men, to be the first-fruits unto God and unto the Lamb." The "first-fruits" were a pledge on the part of the Israelites of other offerings to be made to Jehovah. As the "first-fruits" the one hundred and forty-four thousand are to be thought of as the "pledge" of all the redeemed who are to follow the Lamb upon the earth as history proceeds. Yet other characteristics of these who follow the Lamb which fit them to learn the new song in heaven are seen in this: "And in their mouth was found no lie: they are without blemish."

2. *The tidings of God and the gospel are universal* (14:6-7). —No storm that may break upon the earth can still the proclamation of the good news of redemption in Jesus Christ. The gospel is *eternal good news.* John in this vision sees an angel flying in mid-heaven and proclaiming it as such. The *euangelion,* good news, is for "every nation and tribe and people." And even as men turn from him to worship an earthly ruler, the gospel is offered by God to all unto the end. The appeal comes, "Fear God, and give him glory; for the hour of his judgment is come; and worship him that made the heaven and the earth and sea and fountains of waters." All men may be saved; so long as time lasts, there is opportunity for the most rebellious sinner to turn to God.

3. *Rome's fall is certain; evil cannot prevail* (14:8).—"Fallen, fallen is Babylon the great," cries another angel. The victory of God is assured before the carnage of conflict begins. The wicked city of earth cannot stand.

4. *The doom of those who worship the beast is fixed; the wicked will suffer punishment* (14:9-12).—A third angel gives this assurance. He who worships the beast "shall drink

of the wine of the wrath of God, which is prepared unmixed in the cup of his anger."

5. *The reward of those who die in the Lord is sure* (14:13). —John hears a voice from heaven saying: "Blessed are the dead who die in the Lord from henceforth: yea, saith the Spirit, that they may rest from their labors; for their works follow with them." These would be comforting words to those who faced suffering and death or who had lost loved ones and friends in the persecution of Christians. The works of those who die in the Lord "follow with them"; by which is meant that the deeds done in the name of Christ become a part of the lives of those who do them and thereby survive death in the souls of those who die. Jesus had taught that no one who had given a "little one" even a cup of cold water in his name would lose his reward. Heaven will be a realm where earth's inequalities will be overbalanced with eternal glories.

6. *The Son of man sits in authority as Lord of the harvest upon the earth* (14:14–16).—The vision is of the judgment of God that proceeds apace upon the earth. History moves on inevitably to the harvest and reaping. The harvest need not await the end of time. God is continuously executing judgment among men, separating the righteous from the unrighteous, calling his own to himself and sending the wicked to the place of perdition. Jesus Christ, the great Son of man, is the Lord of this harvest upon the earth. John sees him in his vision as "having on his head a golden crown, and in his hand a sharp sickle." John looks forward and sees the harvest in prospect. "And he that sat on the cloud cast his sickle upon the earth; and the earth was reaped."

It is possible that the vision is of Christ in his second advent. There is some similarity of the picture here with Christ's prediction of his coming given in Mark 13:26 f. The vision is also reminiscent of the explanation of the parable of the tares in Matthew 13:37–43. If this is a vision of the Son of man in his Parousia, the author looks forward to that event without fixing the time of its occurrence.

7. *The consummation of the harvest is the wrath of God*

(*14:17-20*).—John sees in this vision an angel "cast his sickle into the earth." The "vintage of the earth" is gathered and cast "into the winepress, the great *winepress* of the wrath of God. And the winepress was trodden without the city, and there came out blood from the winepress, even unto the bridles of the horses, as far as a thousand and six hundred furlongs." This is a picture of the overflowing wrath of God in store for those who deny his sovereignty and refuse his salvation.

Scene Four

VISION OF THE SEVEN ANGELS WITH THE BOWLS OF THE WRATH OF GOD

(Chapters 15–16)

THE stage is now set for the resumption of the action involving the great conflict between Christ and the Caesars. The two beasts have made their appearance and are ready for the war. In an "interlude" John has given by a series of seven visions assurances and warnings bearing upon the battle that now looms. The scene before us introduces "seven plagues, *which are* the last." These plagues are a representation of the wrath of God, and in this they are similar to the plagues of the visions under the trumpet angels. But the bowl-plagues have their own character and are designed to represent a specific manifestation of God's wrath, as we shall see. The plagues given in the visions under the six trumpet angels, it will be remembered, are limited in their power to destroy. "A third part of the earth" is burned up; "a third part of the sea" becomes blood; the "third part of the sun" was smitten; the "third part of men" was killed. The bowl-plagues, however, are directed without limit against those who are opposed to the sovereignty of God in Christ. They are the supreme and ultimate expression of the wrath of God.

The purpose of the visions of the seven bowls is to reveal the wrath of God as it is manifested specifically against an earthly government which sets itself against the rule of God in Christ. The visions give us a revelation of the coming defeat of the beasts, which, as actors in the drama, are still on the stage flouting the rule of God and compelling the multitudes to pay homage to an earthly ruler as divine. The first plague brings terrible suffering to "the men that had the mark of the beast, and that worshipped his image." The fifth bowl is poured out "upon the throne of the beast," with the result that "his kingdom was darkened." When the seventh bowl is poured out, "the great city was divided into three parts, and the cities of the nations fell; and Babylon the great was remembered in the sight of God, to give unto her the cup of the wine of the fierceness of his wrath." "Babylon," of course, represents the city of Rome, as is clearly indicated in the visions of chapters 17 and 18, and particularly 17:9 where the harlot, which is Babylon, is pictured as sitting on seven mountains, patently an allusion to the fact that Rome was built upon seven hills. And so the bowls are designed to show how the wrath of God will operate in all its fierceness to bring about the doom of Rome and of the reign of the first beast. Here it should be said that Rome itself is a symbol. Although the author foresaw and predicted the fall of Rome itself, the city is a figure of the wicked metropolis of earth which stands over against the City of God, the new Jerusalem. The wicked city of earth, be it Rome or some other, remains ever an object of the fierce wrath of God. This is certainly a teaching that may be found by implication in the visions of the seven bowls.

Preparation in Heaven for the Pouring Out of the Bowls.—Chapter 15

John introduces the new series of visions in these words: "And I saw another sign in heaven, great and marvellous, seven angels having seven plagues, which are the last, for in them is finished the wrath of God."

Again we must face the question as to whether the author is looking to the end of the age. Are these plagues of the seven bowls intended to represent a series of woes leading up to the Parousia and the end of time? The language with which they are introduced would on its face suggest this; the plagues are called "the last," and it is said that "in them is finished the wrath of God." But this conclusion cannot stand upon the language alone. An exploration of the relationship of this series of visions to the larger context of the whole drama and to the author's purpose will show that it is not necessary to interpret the bowls of wrath as representing eschatological events.

In the first place it should be said that if these plagues represent woes of the last days, they are symbols of *supernatural* events which in the thinking of the author were actually to take place in history. The woes of the "last days" are conceived of by apocalyptic-minded interpreters as supernatural happenings sent by God upon the earth. Now it is difficult indeed to believe that John would conceive of any such happenings as are described in these visions as literally taking place in history. Why should we demand that symbols here be turned into actual happenings that reproduce literally the action of visions when this demand is not made of the symbolism in other parts of the book? To be sure, John uses symbols to represent actual men and events, and from time to time it has been possible to designate the persons and events indicated by the symbols. But in such cases the individuals suggested by the symbols are understood to be *men*, and the events are understood to be actual *historical* events. For instance, the head of the first beast "smitten unto death" in 13:3 is Nero, a real person, and the "worship of the beast" in 13:12 represents the practice of emperor worship, something which actually took place in the first century. Now it is true that John also uses symbols to represent action that has no real facsimile in history. An instance of this is the breaking of the seals of the scroll by the Lamb. But in the use of symbolism to represent an action of this sort, it is always apparent that the symbol or the picture is of some great spiritual reality which, though it is not literally acted out in history as por-

154

trayed by the symbolism, is nevertheless true as a spiritual reality.

As we return to the symbolism of the bowls, is it not apparent that John expected no literal reproduction of the action in these visions? Are we to believe, for instance, that when in his vision he saw the second bowl poured out, he saw what he believed was actually to take place, namely, that "the sea became blood as of a dead man; and every living soul died, even the things that were in the sea"? It is far more reasonable to think that a man so rich in intelligence and insight as was the Seer of Patmos was not so naive as this but was fully conscious of the fact that here and elsewhere when he used symbolism of this kind he employed it to represent *spiritual truth and reality*. These plagues, as we have suggested, are symbols of the wrath of God reserved for that earthly government which is opposed to the sovereignty of God in Jesus Christ. The plagues do not represent *supernatural* events; hence, they cannot be those woes which some apocalyptic writers seem to picture as taking place in history in connection with the end of the world.

Now we may adduce additional evidence for the view that these are not the woes of the "last days." As has been suggested, the series of seven bowls is designed to point to the fall of Rome. The pouring out of the seventh and climactic bowl is the signal for the announcement, "Babylon the great was remembered in the sight of God, to give unto her the cup of the wine of the fierceness of his wrath," and immediately there follows the series of visions depicting the judgment and fall of Rome. Now how is Rome to be destroyed? Is it by some great supernatural event? This is not the prediction that is given by John. The prophecy that is given in 17:16–17 indicates that the city will be laid low by traitorous friends, the beast, and his puppet allies, "the ten horns." Here we read: "And the ten horns which thou sawest, and the beast, these shall hate the harlot, and shall make her desolate and naked, and shall eat her flesh, and shall burn her utterly with fire. For God did put in their hearts to do his mind, and to

155

come to one mind, and to give their kingdom unto the beast, until the words of God should be accomplished." According to this prediction the fall of Rome would be accomplished by quite natural means. Her would-be friends would become her enemies and destroy her. There was historical precedent for John's prediction. The emperor Nero had burned the city. But we shall give fuller attention to this prophecy and its fulfilment in its proper place. Here we emphasize the fact that the bowl plagues cannot represent supernatural events, since Rome's fall is not to be accomplished in the thinking of John by a supernatural event; and if they are not supernatural events, they are not woes of the "last days."

There is this other consideration in favor of the position we have taken: John represents Christians as being in the city of Rome as the plagues come upon her, or as they are about to descend upon the city. In 18:4 there is this warning: "Come forth, my people, out of her, that ye have no fellowship with her sins, and that ye receive not of her plagues." Now it is reasonable to believe that the people of God could not be caught in the so-called "last plagues." It is generally assumed by interpreters who hold to the view that there will be great woes in the last days, sent supernaturally upon the world by God, that God's people will be safe from the ravages of these woes. But here in John's vision the people of God must be warned to flee from the wicked city in order to escape the plagues that are to come. The implication is that they could be destroyed by them simply by remaining in the city. It is unreasonable to suppose that God would send by a supernatural act final plagues upon the earth which would expose his own people to destruction. It would appear here that we have the representation of a natural happening in history in relation to which Christians are called upon to exercise human wisdom as participants in actual historical events.

Why, then, are these plagues called the "last," and why is it said "in them is finished the wrath of God"? These plagues are "last" in that there can be no expression of the wrath of God in degree beyond its direction toward a heathen world government such as that of the Caesars which denies the sovereignty of God in Christ. In these plagues is "finished" (or "completed" as the Greek verb *teleo* may be translated) the wrath of God in that the ultimate expression of his wrath is this expression against godless Rome and the Caesars with their blasphemous claims of divinity.

In his vision John sees preparation for these plagues somewhat after the manner of the preparation that was made for the plagues that were revealed in the series of the six trumpet angels of chapter 8. In the preparation for the sounding of the trumpets, the action is initiated before the throne of God, and an angel adds incense "to the prayers of all the saints upon the golden altar." We return to the great Court of Heaven for the initiation of this series of plagues. "And I saw as it were a sea of glass mingled with fire," says John, "and them that come off victorious from the beast, and from his image, and from the number of his name, standing by the sea of glass, having harps of God. And they sing the song of Moses the servant of God, and the song of the Lamb."

What is the song of Moses? There are commentators who take it to be the song sung by the Israelites to signalize their crossing of the Red Sea and victory over the Egyptians recorded in Exodus 15. Other commentators take it to be the song that Moses taught the Israelites before his death, found in the thirty-second chapter of Deuteronomy. The brief "song" found here in the vision of Revelation 15:3-4 comes nearer being an epitome of the latter than of the former. The purpose of the song here seems to be the justification of the action of God in expressing his wrath, as the plagues of the bowls will represent him as expressing it. "Righteous and true are thy ways" is a line from this "song." Returning to the song of Moses in Deuteronomy 32, we find that immediately prior to the giving of it by Moses to the assembly of Israel, Moses commanded the Levites to place the book of the law by the side of the ark of the covenant "that it may be there for a witness against thee." Moses then predicts that in days to come the people will "utterly corrupt" themselves to

157

"provoke" Jehovah "to anger through the work of your hands." In the vision of Revelation, John says, after his recital of the song, "I saw, and the temple of the tabernacle of the testimony in heaven was opened." The temple in heaven, if we hark back to 11:19, contained the ark of the covenant. Presumably, therefore, there is a reminiscence here of the Old Testament scene in which the song is given from the tabernacle and before the ark of God. The song in heaven is given from the heavenly sanctuary. It echoes the song of Moses in that it extols God for his justice and praises him for the expression of his wrath. A passage from Moses' song declares: "If I whet my glittering sword, and my hand take hold on judgment; I will render vengeance to mine adversaries, and will recompense them that hate me. I will make mine arrows drunk with blood, and my sword shall devour flesh; with the blood of the slain and the captives, from the head of the leaders of the enemy. Rejoice, O ye nations, with his people: for he will avenge the blood of his servants, and will render vengeance to his adversaries, and will make expiation for his land, for his people" (Deuteronomy 32:41–43). Thus it would seem that the circumstances point to this song of Moses as being the background of the "song of Moses the servant of God, and the song of the Lamb." A terrible expression of the wrath of God is to be revealed. John vindicates this expression of wrath before the visions are given of the pouring out of the bowls. The Lamb is made to join with Moses, as it were, in justifying this extreme manifestation of God's wrath upon his enemies.

Pouring Out of the Bowls.—Chapter 16

There is some similarity between the bowl plagues and the ten plagues sent by Jehovah upon Egypt. As in the case of the Egyptian plagues, a wicked world ruler and his subjects are the objects of God's wrath in the pouring out of the bowls. And, as in the case of the unrepentant Pharaoh, the bowl plagues fail to work repentance in the hearts of the enemies

158

THE GREAT DRAMA—ACT TWO

of God. When, in the fourth plague, the bowl is poured out
upon the sun and men are "scorched with great heat," they
blaspheme "the name of God who hath the power over these
plagues; and they repented not to give him glory." When the
fifth angel pours his bowl upon the throne of the beast, it is
said that "his kingdom was darkened: and they gnawed their
tongues for pain, and they blasphemed the god of heaven
because of their pains and their sores; and they repented not
of their works." As a result of the first plague, the earth
"became a noisome and grievous sore upon the men that had
the mark of the beast, and that worshipped his image." This
is reminiscent of the plague of boils which was sent upon the
Egyptians, described in Exodus 9:8–12. The third bowl
plague echoes the first Egyptian plague, which turned the
waters into blood (Exodus 7:20–25). The pouring of the
seventh bowl brings a great downpour of huge hailstones
from the sky. This is reminiscent of the plague of hail upon
Egypt (Exodus 9:22–26).

The sixth bowl plague echoes the plague of the sixth
trumpet angel in 9:13–21. In that plague armies of horsemen
are represented as coming from the region of the Euphrates,
the region from which Israel's captors had come. The sixth
angel in this series pours his bowl "upon the great river, the
river Euphrates." This dried up the river and "made ready
for the kings that came from the sunrising." But this plague
points specifically to the great battle that looms between the
beast and his allies and Christ and his army. The place of
the battle is called Har-Magedon. The pouring out of this
sixth bowl has the effect of stirring up the "kings of the whole
world, to gather them together unto the war of the great day
of God, the Almighty." This is accomplished by means of
"three unclean spirits, as it were frogs" that come "out of the
mouth of the dragon, and out of the mouth of the beast, and
out of the mouth of the false prophet." This is a picture in
symbols of the power of Satan (the dragon), the emperor or
the succession of emperors (the beast), and the priests of
the emperor cult (the false prophet) to deceive the various

159

dependent principalities and kingdoms of the empire to join in the warfare of the empire against Christianity. The "war of the great day of God, the Almighty," which is to be fought out at Har-Magedon is the battle between Christ and his army and the beast and his allies described in 19:17–21. This is not the final conflict in which "Gog and Magog" figure (20:8–9), a conflict that does not take place until "the thousand years are finished" (20:7). What is represented by the term "Har-Magedon," or, as it is written in the Authorized Version, "Armageddon"? It seems to be a compound of the Hebrew words *har*, "mountain," and *Megidon* (Greek, *Mageddōn*, or *Magedōn*), a proper name standing for "the stronghold in the valley of Esdraelon near which, 'by the waters of Megiddo' (Judges 5:19), Israel gained a decisive victory over the kings of Canaan—a victory celebrated forever afterwards in the song of Deborah, Judges chapt. 5 "[1] The plain of Esdraelon was the scene of several great battles and would serve handily as a symbol of the place of the great battle between the army of Christ and the hosts of the Caesars and their allies. Here Josiah suffered his disastrous defeat at the hands of Pharaoh Necho of Egypt. According to Swete, this event "burnt itself into the memory of the Jewish people, and the mourning for Josiah in the valley of Megiddo was long afterwards quoted as a typical instance of national grief (Zech. 12:11). Thus Megiddo fitly symbolizes the world-wide distress of the nations at the overthrow of their kings in the final war."[2] The vision of the sixth plague is designed, therefore, to show how the great battle between Christ and his army and Satan's hosts shaped up. It is brought about as a result of the demonic influence (16:14) of Satan, the emperor, and the priests of the emperor cult.

The seventh plague is the climactic plague of the series. It symbolizes the setting in motion of those forces which result in the destruction of the wicked city of earth, Babylon, or

---

[1] *The Apocalypse of John*, by Isbon T. Beckwith; New York: the Macmillan Co., 1919, page 685.

[2] *Apocalypse of St. John*, p. 209.

Rome. The vision is a revelation of the certain defeat, not only of Rome, but also of "the cities of the nations" (or of "the Gentiles"). When the seventh bowl is poured out, "the great city was divided into three parts, and the cities of the nations fell: and Babylon the great was remembered in the sight of God, to give unto her the cup of the wine of the fierceness of his wrath."

By further comparison of the series of seven trumpet-angels in chapters 8, 9, and 11 with the series of the angels of the bowls, we shall discover a very significant contrast which is designed to show in bold relief the contrast between the reign of God in Christ and the fate of the city of earth. This comes to light in the vision of the pouring out of the seventh bowl. The vision of the seventh bowl is to be viewed against the vision of the seventh trumpet angel. The first series of seven is climaxed by the great proclamation that "the sovereignty over the world became our Lord's and his Christ's, and he shall reign for ever and ever." Now this assertion of the everlasting reign of Christ comes following the series of plagues that are revealed with the blowing of the six trumpets. At the end of this series of plagues there is the proclamation of God's great rule in Christ. But now, in the climax of the series of the seven bowls, by way of contrast, the case is vastly different with the wicked city of earth and "the cities of the nations." Here is pictured disaster for the powers of earth that challenge the sovereignty of God in Christ. The contrast suggests that, notwithstanding the visitation of wrath upon the earth, the rule of Christ remains secure, established forever, whereas the manifestation of God's wrath against the powers of earth issues inevitably in their downfall.

Another feature of the representation of the wrath of God under the pouring out of these bowls is to be observed. This is the added justification the series presents of the expression of God's wrath. It was observed that "the song of Moses, the servant of God, and the song of the Lamb" in 15:3–4 is given as a vindication of the manifestation of God's wrath which is in prospect as the seven angels prepare to pour out the bowls.

161

This vindication is strongly supported by revelations that come to John when he sees in his vision the third bowl poured out. He says: "And I heard the angel of the waters saying, Righteous art thou, who art and who wast, thou Holy One, because thou didst thus judge: for they poured out the blood of saints and prophets, and blood hast thou given them to drink: they are worthy. And I heard the altar saying, Yea, O Lord God, the Almighty, true and righteous are thy judgments." In both the song of Moses and the Lamb and these statements in the vision of the pouring out of the third bowl, the wrath of God is based in the holiness of God. In the former is heard the cry, "Who shall not fear, O Lord, and glorify thy name? for thou art holy." In the latter the angel of the waters declares, "Righteous art thou, who art and who wast, thou Holy One, because thou didst thus judge."

These statements give us some hint as to the practical aspects of the manifestation of the wrath of God as it is seen in the visions of Revelation, and it is well to pause at this point to inquire into the meaning of the wrath of God as it is symbolized in these visions of the pouring out of the bowls. If these great plagues are not conceived of as supernatural happenings, how are they to be conceived? Is it possible that they represent historical forces which are capable of expressing the fierce wrath of God symbolized in these visions?

By way of reply to these questions, let us first repeat that this series of visions represents the wrath of God as based in his holiness. Now God, as the holy God, must of necessity express his displeasure against sin continuously. The expression of his wrath cannot be arbitrary; he is the just God. It is therefore necessary as a concomitant to his holiness that there be an expression of his displeasure against sin that conforms to his character as the holy God. The vindication of his character as the holy God cannot await the final judgment. God will bring about his own will in the world before life on this planet ceases. The whole concept of God's relationship to man and history is involved in the manifestation of his wrath. If God has dealings at all with man, if there is action and

162

reaction in history in which God is involved at all, the relationship thus shown between God and man and history must of necessity exhibit God as he is from eternity. God is from eternity the holy God; therefore, his relations to men and history must exhibit his wrath. The demand that is raised by the character of God is met in his moral order. This moral order which he has created perpetually expresses his holiness and his wrath.

The apostle Paul affirmed the existence of this moral order in his statement, "Be not deceived; God is not mocked: for whatsoever a man soweth, that shall he also reap. For he that soweth unto his own flesh shall of the flesh reap corruption; but he that soweth unto the Spirit shall of the Spirit reap eternal life" (Galatians 6:7–8). Paul did not conceive of the reaping as held back in its operation until the final judgment; he believed that man belonged to a moral cosmos which carried its laws of punishment for sin and reward for righteousness—laws which continuously operated in the present life of humanity. This same truth is also advanced by Paul in Romans 1:18: "For the wrath of God is being revealed [*apokaluptetai*, progressive or customary present] from heaven against all ungodliness and unrighteousness of men, who hinder the truth in unrighteousness." The context from which this statement is taken reveals Paul's belief in the moral cosmos which continually manifests the wrath of God and exacts punishment for the infringement of its laws. Three times Paul repeats the formula, "God gave them up" (Romans 1:24,26,28), as applying to that segment of humanity which worshiped idols and refused to obey the true God who had manifested himself to them. These idolaters became the victims of "the lusts of their hearts," their "vile passions," "a reprobate mind," etc. This Paul interpreted as the operation of the wrath of God.

Now is it unreasonable to say that John believed in this same moral cosmos in which Paul believed, and described in his own way the operation of the same wrath which Paul explains in Romans and Galatians? We think not. A reasonable interpretation of the visions of the bowls of wrath is that they represent the effects of the wrath of God expressed through historical conditions and events to bring about the disintegration and downfall of the pagan world power that challenged the sovereignty of God in Christ through imperial Rome. This is substantiated by the circumstance to which attention has been directed, namely, that John depicts the downfall of Rome as effected through a coalition of the imperial power and the "ten horns," or subject kingdoms (17:16 f).

This interpretation of the wrath of God as revealed in the visions of the bowls is not to exclude the truth that the historical manifestation of the wrath of God prefigures the consummation of the wrath in the world to come. In the New Testament no sharp division is to be made between the earthly and final expression of God's wrath. The wrath which is displayed in history is to be thought of as having its ultimate consummation in the final judgment. Therefore, every exhibition of God's wrath in history is a foretaste of the wrath to come.

If we seek for some illustration in our own time of the certain and continuous operation of the wrath of God in history against a people who turned from God to deify its own rulers, we may find that illustration in the case of Germany. If there be any doubt that the wrath of God as illustrated in the pouring out of the bowls could be expressed in history by natural means, let the terrible destruction and carnage visited upon Nazi Germany and the downfall of this once proud state serve as the answer to the doubt! Nazi Germany deified Hitler and made nazism a religion, paralleling rather closely the action of the ancient Roman Empire in deifying the emperor and making a religion out of emperor worship. This is not to place upon Germany all the blame for World War II, nor is it to solve all the mysteries connected with the suffering of the innocent as a result of that conflict. It seems significant, however, that two nations in that conflict, Germany and Japan, which deified their rulers lost their

164

sovereignty as nations. It might be pointed out here that there has been no sovereignty in history which has successfully challenged the sovereignty of God in Jesus Christ. Might this not be considered a token of the fact that there will never be in history a nation which will successfully challenge that sovereignty?

This final circumstance in connection with the visions of the bowls should not be overlooked: The expression of God's wrath is a vindication of the sufferings and death of his people. With the breaking of the fifth seal of the scroll taken by the Lamb from the hand of God, there was a cry from the souls of those "underneath the altar" who had been "slain for the word of God and for the testimony which they held." This cry was: "How long, O Master, the holy and true, dost thou not judge and avenge our blood on them that dwell on the earth?" (6:10). When the third bowl is poured out, there is given a dramatic sequel to this cry. John says, "And I heard the altar saying, Yea, O Lord God, the Almighty, true and righteous are thy judgments." Thus does John indicate that the expression of God's wrath against the ungodly world powers will vindicate the saints in the shedding of their blood and in the surrender of their lives in the cause of Christ. Thus are we reminded that the sacrifices of God's people are vindicated, not only at the final judgment, but also in the present world. Those who have the eyes to see may observe such vindication continually manifested in history. The death that comes to a nation which rejects God is visible evidence that the better way chosen by men who serve God even unto death is much more to be desired than the way of the ungodly.

Scene Five

JUDGMENT OF BABYLON (ROME) AND PROCLAMATION OF HER DOOM

(Chapters 17:1 to 19:5)

THE certain doom of the wicked city of earth has been foretold in the visions of the bowls of God's wrath. The pouring out of the bowls has moved swiftly and climactically toward the ultimate expression of the wrath of God in the bringing low of Rome which is called Babylon. It remains now for the Seer to identify Babylon, to describe the fateful events leading up to her fall and to give an account of her destruction.

Vision and Interpretation of the Great Harlot.—Chapter 17

John thinks of the wicked city of earth as a great harlot. He is invited by one of the angels who poured out the bowls of wrath to come and see "the judgment of the great harlot that sitteth upon many waters; with whom the kings of the earth committed fornication, and they that dwell in the earth were made drunken with the wine of her fornication." There is the implication here that these kings of the earth have turned aside from allegiance to God, the true and rightful sovereign, to subject themselves to the wicked sovereignty of this sinful harlot. There is now given a picture which provides one of those vivid contrasts so often found in Revelation. John says that the angel carried him "away in the Spirit into

166

a wilderness." There he saw "a woman sitting upon a scarlet-colored beast, full of names of blasphemy, having seven heads and ten horns." The contrast is to be seen by comparing this picture with the vision seen by the Seer later on when one of the angels of the seven bowl plagues said to him, "Come hither, I will show thee the bride, the wife of the Lamb" (21:9). In obedience to this command, John is carried away "in the Spirit to a mountain great and high." There he sees "the holy city Jerusalem, coming down out of heaven from God, having the glory of God" (21:10). Thus is the vision of the mountain contrasted with the vision seen in the wilderness; thus is the City of God set over against the wicked city of earth.

The woman is arrayed in clothes befitting the character of the harlot that she is. Her apparel is rich and gaudy, and in her hand she holds a wine cup with which to tempt her lovers. It is "full of abominations, even the unclean things of her fornication." This woman has her name written upon her forehead, this being perhaps a reflection of a custom practiced by the prostitutes of the day to wear their names appended on their foreheads. Her name is "Mystery, Babylon the Great, the Mother of the Harlots and of the Abominations of the earth." Swete says at this point: "The Woman on the Beast represents, is the symbol of, Babylon the Great, while Babylon itself is a mystical name for the city which is now the mistress of the world. Her gaily attired, jewelled, gilded person, and her cup of abominations, proclaim her to be the Mother-Harlot of the Earth. All the *pornai* of all the subject races are her children; all the vices and superstitions of the provinces were suckled at her breasts. The *metropolis* of the Empire is the source and fountain-head of its impurities, the mother of harlots, even as the Church is the mother of Christ and His Saints (12:5,17). The maternal character of Rome was recognized by the provincials themselves as late as the end of the fourth century, but from a different point of view."[1] The harlot is drunk but not with wine; her intoxica-

[1]*The Apocalypse of St. John*, p. 217.

tion has been caused by drinking the blood of the saints. Thus does John trace the martyr death of the Christians in the provinces to a policy formulated in the capital city.

And now John proceeds to give by revelations that come to him from the angel a series of identifications or explanations designed to assist his readers to understand his symbolism. A portion of his explanation is clear enough, but we can only guess at the meaning of the riddle of the "seven kings" and the "beast that was, and is not," etc., in 17:10–11.

The first clue that John gives to the meaning of his symbolism is this: "The beast that thou sawest was, and is not; and is about to come up out of the abyss, and to go into perdition." This beast, which has seven heads, seems to be the same beast of 13:1. There is no reason to interpret the symbolism otherwise. This beast therefore represents the emperors or the imperial power. The statement that this beast "was, and is not" is another way of using the Nero *redivivus* myth. In 13:3 the beast is described as having a head which had been "smitten unto" death but had been healed. Here again, then, John is warning his readers that the imperial Roman power is to become Nero-incarnate; the worst of the emperors is to come alive, as it were, and dwell in the reigning Caesar. Doubtless John sees this beast, as was previously suggested, as the Antichrist. But his downfall is predicted: he will "go into perdition." John gives to his readers a compliment by way of implication in the statement of verse 8: "And they that dwell on the earth shall wonder, they whose name hath not been written in the book of life from the foundation of the world, when they behold the beast, how that he was, and is not, and shall come." This is as if to say: "The blind pagans will not understand my language, but you who are Christians will understand; you will know that this symbolism represents the Antichrist sitting on the throne of the empire in Rome in the person of an emperor inspired by the spirit of Nero."

John now proceeds with his riddle: "Here is the mind that hath wisdom. The seven heads are seven mountains, on which the woman sitteth: and they are seven kings; the five are fallen, the one is, the other is not yet come; and when he cometh, he must continue a little while. And the beast that was, and is not, is himself also an eighth, and is of the seven; and he goeth into perdition."

The meaning of the first part of the riddle is obvious, but the same cannot be said for the remaining part of it. The seven heads of the beast are made to represent both the city of Rome and "seven kings." The "seven mountains" obviously refer to the seven hills upon which ancient Rome was built. The harlot sits then, not only upon these seven hills, that is, upon the city of Rome, but upon the heads of these kings. The kings clearly represent a succession of emperors, and the city of Rome is represented as being sustained by this succession of emperors. We can only guess at the remainder of the riddle. In the first place, we cannot know whether John intended by the symbolism to designate certain emperors or merely to represent the imperial power or the succession of emperors. On the assumption that he had specific emperors in mind, we can suggest a solution of the riddle. If we can begin with the Emperor Tiberius, under whom Christ was crucified, and if we are permitted to omit from the list of emperors the three men who succeeded Nero but together reigned for approximately one year, it is possible to offer a fairly reasonable interpretation of the riddle. The interpretation is as follows:

"They are seven kings."—Tiberius (A.D. 14–37); Caligula (A.D. 37–41); Claudius (A.D. 41–54); Nero (A.D. 54–68); Vespasian (A.D. 69–79); Titus (A.D. 79–81); Domitian (A.D. 81–96). The three men who are omitted from the list, Galba, Otho, and Vitellius, who were in power in succession so briefly after Nero's death, were not actually looked upon as emperors.

"The five are fallen."—Tiberius, Caligula, Claudius, Vespasian, and Titus. Nero is omitted here because in the riddle he is regarded as "coming alive" and therefore as not fallen. This would bring the time of the writing of the Revelation to a period beyond Titus' reign, since Titus was "fallen."

"The one is."—Domitian. This emperor succeeds Titus, and his being alive at the time of the writing of Revelation fits the conditions of the internal evidence of the book.

"The other is not yet come; and when he cometh, he must continue a little while."—This is Nero come alive to reincarnate himself in a reigning emperor. The fact that he is to continue only "a little while" identifies him with the beast of 17:8 that comes up out of the abyss, but which is "to go into perdition." It is to be remembered that this beast also represents the succession of emperors.

"And the beast that was, and is not, is himself also an eighth, and is of the seven; and he goeth into perdition."—Again, this is Nero come to life, the symbol of the Antichrist. Because Nero had reigned as a living emperor, he would be "of the seven"; but in that he was to return, as it were, to become emperor again, he "is himself also an eighth."

Now it is not clear from the riddle whether the author intended to predict that in Domitian the spirit of Nero would be so truly reincarnated that he could be designated Antichrist, or to leave it as a possibility that an emperor in the immediate future after Domitian would fill this role. It is entirely possible that John saw Domitian as the incarnation of Nero and, therefore, as the Antichrist. By his persecution of the Christians and his insistence on being paid divine honors, it is certainly not unreasonable to identify him as the seventh in the line of emperors, inspired by the demonic spirit of Nero, who was "of the seven" but who was also "an eighth."

John proceeds to explain that "the ten horns that thou sawest are ten kings, who have received no kingdom as yet; but they receive authority as kings, with the beast, for one hour. These have one mind, and they give their power and authority unto the beast." Apparently this is a representation of puppet kings and dependencies that owed their allegiance to Rome and the Caesars. John tells us at this point that these puppet rulers and the beast "shall war against the Lamb, and the Lamb shall overcome them, for he is Lord of lords, and

King of kings; and they *also shall overcome* that are with him, called chosen and faithful." It is worth while to observe that the Lamb is referred to here *before the coming great battle* as "Lord of lords, and King of kings." This would suggest that John thinks of Christ as King from the time of his exaltation to the right hand of the Father after the completion of his earthly ministry.

"The waters which thou sawest, where the harlot sitteth" is now interpreted. These waters, explains the Seer, "are peoples, and multitudes, and nations, and tongues." This is a reference to 17:1 where the harlot was introduced as one that "sitteth upon many waters." This is a vivid and suggestive picture of Rome as drawing her sustenance from the entire empire. Through conquest many peoples and nations had been made tributary to Rome. These poured their treasures into the great city. It is a historical fact that Rome was dependent upon the outside world for her very existence. Without the grain that Egypt supplied, for instance, her people would have starved. Exploitation of conquered provinces had produced a number of rich and powerful families in Rome and had filled the city with wealth and luxury. It has been estimated that in the time of Claudius there were as many slaves as freemen in the city of Rome. According to another estimate there were 650,000 slaves in the city in 5 B.C.

John concludes his interpretation with these words: "And the ten horns which thou sawest, and the beast, these shall hate the harlot, and shall make her desolate and naked, and shall eat her flesh, and shall burn her utterly with fire. For God did put in their hearts to do his mind, and to give their kingdom [reign, dominion] unto the beast, until the words of God should be accomplished. And the woman whom thou sawest is the great city, which reigneth over the kings of the earth."

By these words, as has been suggested, the Seer predicts the downfall of Rome at the hands of her own rulers in league with dependent powers. This is a picture of the fall of the city as the result of internal troubles and disintegration.

There was precedent for such a prediction. Nero had burned the city in A.D. 64. The city was "twice the scene of carnage and plunder" in the year A.D. 69, as Swete points out. Commenting further on this prophecy, Swete says: "Domitian had no obvious heir, and his life was menaced by conspiracies; at any moment Rome might be sacked again. But, St. John looks beyond the end of Domitian's reign to a future which he does not attempt to fix. He has a pre-vision of forces within the Empire taking shape under the leadership of men who, without the Imperial purple, would possess Imperial powers, and would use them for the destruction of Rome. His forecast was verified by the long series of disasters sustained at the hands of Alaric, Genseric, Ricimer, Totila, the representatives of the hordes which overran the West in the 5th and 6th centuries; not to mention later sieges by less barbarous foes. No reader of the *Decline and Fall* can be at a loss for materials which will at once illustrate and justify the general trend of St. John's prophecy."[2]

Here, we may say again, is the wrath of God in action. Rome would fall because she disregarded the laws of God's moral cosmos. These laws, expressing the holiness of God, would exact full penalty for her sins and the sins of her people. God would utilize men, conditions, and events in the historical process to manifest his wrath. In such manner does the wrath of God ever work to exact justice in the earth.

→

Sevenfold Proclamation of Judgment Upon the Great Harlot.—18:1 to 19:5

The prophet proceeds now to give in vivid detail a description of the coming destruction of Rome. In his dramatic way he tells his story as if the action is in progress. The passage reveals a rather remarkable knowledge on the part of the author of the commerce and trade which flowed in and out of Rome and made the city the center of the economic life of the ancient world.

[2]*Ibid.*, p. 225.

The first pronouncement of doom upon the city comes from an angel from heaven "having great authority." He cries out, "Fallen, fallen is Babylon the great, and is become a habitation of demons, and a hold of every unclean spirit, and a hold of every unclean and hateful bird." The words are an echo of Isaiah's pronouncement of doom upon ancient Babylon (Isaiah 21:9). The aorists in the Greek (*epesen, epesen,* "fallen, fallen") present the action as if it were done. Demons were thought by the ancients to inhabit empty and deserted buildings. Here the city's emptiness and her deserted houses are emphasized by the reference to demons inhabiting the city.

The next pronouncement of doom comes from "another voice from heaven" which first warns God's people to withdraw from the wicked city and have no complicity in her sins. This "voice" predicts that "in one day shall her plagues come, death, and mourning, and famine; and she shall be utterly burned with fire; for strong is the Lord God who judged her."

Yet again is the doom of the city indicated. Now it appears in a lament that comes from the "kings of the earth" who "committed fornication" with the wicked city. They wail, "Woe, woe, the great city, Babylon, the strong city! for in one hour is thy judgment come."

Now the merchants of the earth join the chorus of those bewailing the fate of the once proud city. The description given of their lament contains an extraordinary list of the articles of trade imported into the city. There is a touch of humor in the author's description of the merchants standing "afar off" as they watch the burning of the city "for the fear of her torment." But they add to the pronouncements of doom with the words, "In one hour so great riches is made desolate."

The men of the sea, the shipmasters and the sailors, contribute their sorrowful wail. "Woe, woe," they cry, "the great city wherein all that had their ships in the sea were made rich by reason of her costliness! for in one hour is she made desolate."

173

The sixth pronouncement of doom is made by a "strong angel" who "took up a stone as it were a great millstone and cast it into the sea, saying, Thus with a mighty fall shall Babylon, the great city, be cast down, and shall be found no more at all."

The final pronouncement of doom upon the wicked city of earth issues from heaven (19:1–5). The Seer hears "a great voice of a great multitude in heaven, saying, Hallelujah; Salvation, and glory, and power, belong to our God: for true and righteous are his judgments; for he hath judged the great harlot, her that corrupted the earth with her fornication, and he hath avenged the blood of his servants at her hand." Thus heaven witnesses to the destruction of the corrupt city and praises God for the manifestation of his wrath to bring her low.

Thus does the author see in his mind's eye the destruction of the city of the beast and the fountainhead of that evil power that had proceeded forth into the world to bring persecution and death to the saints of God. It is not necessary to think that John believed his prophecy would be fulfilled literally in the manner in which he has described the city's destruction. It is sufficient to believe that he foresaw future sufferings, troubles, and woes that would issue in her downfall and disappearance as a world power. We know that the fall of Rome thus interpreted came to pass.

This dramatic recital of the fall of Rome will be the better appreciated when viewed in contrast with the description yet to come of the City of God, the New Jerusalem. Even as the doom of the wicked city of earth is proclaimed seven times over, the action begins to move toward the revealing of the Perfect City, the "city coming down out of heaven from God," whose perfection will be glowingly recited in the description of her seven matchless characteristics. As we see the city of earth die, we are granted a vision of the City of God "coming down out of heaven from God, made ready as a bride adorned for her husband."

Scene Six

THE VICTORY OF CHRIST OVER SATAN AND THE BEAST

(Chapters 19:6 to 20:10)

THE action of the Great Drama of the Sovereignty of God in Christ moves swiftly on to its grand climax. The opposing characters are all now clearly defined. From the moment of the birth of the Man Child, it was apparent that conflict was inevitable. With that birth there was aroused the undying antagonism of the dragon who is the great Accuser of men. The stage was set for combat to the death in the dragon's commission of the two beasts as his representatives on earth. The Man Child, who is also the Lamb, becomes the Messiah of God to lead the people of God in their contest with the two beasts. The great harlot, who is the city of the first beast, has appeared upon the stage to hear the sentence of her doom. And now the final battle between Messiah, who is the Christ, and the beast with his allies draws quickly on. It is this final struggle, which is within history, that now engages the attention of the Seer of Patmos as he draws back the curtain once more to reveal to us the things that are to come.

Announcement of the Marriage Supper of the Lamb.—19:6–10

This scene opens with a mighty chorus of praise. At once we recognize the notes that strike our ears as being exultant,

175

triumphant. "And I heard as it were the voice of a great multitude, and as the voice of many waters, and as the voice of mighty thunders, saying, Hallelujah: for the Lord our God, the Almighty, reigneth." We can sense in this grand song of exultation the projection into the action of the thrill of victories to come. The great event that calls forth the praise of the heavenly multitudes is the marriage of the Lamb. The voice which John hears continues: "Let us rejoice and be exceeding glad, and let us give glory unto him: for the marriage of the Lamb is come, and his wife hath made herself ready."

What is meant by "the marriage of the Lamb," and when, in the thinking of John, does the marriage take place? These are questions which demand answer before we proceed with the vision. The marriage of the Lamb has to do with the union of Christ with his people, or the church. The "wife" of the Lamb is not precisely identified here, but it is said, "And it was given unto her that she should array herself in fine linen, bright and pure: for the fine linen is the righteous acts of the saints." The "righteous acts of the saints" can be "worn" only by the saints; hence, it is quite clear that the "wife" of the Lamb is the saints. But in 21:9–10, where the Seer describes the invitation to come and see "the bride, the wife of the Lamb," it is obvious that the "bride" is the New Jerusalem. However, there need be no contradiction here. The New Jerusalem is conceived of in one sense as the redeemed saints of God in their glorified state beyond history. Therefore, we can say that the "bride" or the "wife" of the Lamb is all the people of God, living and dead, or the church, the church being conceived of as all the redeemed of all time.

This concept of the church as the bride of Christ is found in Paul's letter to the Ephesians. In this epistle, which was first circulated in the churches of Asia, Paul says: "Wives, be in subjection unto your own husbands, as unto the Lord. For the husband is the head of the wife, as Christ also is the head of the church, being himself the saviour of the body" (Ephesians 5:22–23). And then, as if to suggest that the church was

176

a bride who must keep herself pure that she might be worthy of a consummation of the marriage yet to be, Paul says further: "Husbands, love your wives, even as Christ also loved the church, and gave himself up for it; that he might sanctify it, having cleansed it by the washing of water with the word, that he might present the church to himself a glorious church, not having spot or wrinkle or any such thing; but that it should be holy and without blemish."

Thus this concept of the church as the bride of Christ is a Pauline idea that has been incorporated into the theology of the author of the Apocalypse. The idea was well known in the circle of the churches of Asia, since Paul labored for so long at Ephesus, and since, as we have said, the Epistle to the Ephesians had its first currency among the churches of Asia. There is a marked consistency between Paul's and John's use of the concept. In Ephesians the bride is to be prepared for the consummation of the marriage by the preservation of her purity; she is not to have "spot or wrinkle or any such thing," but she is to be "holy and without blemish." In Revelation, in preparation for the marriage to the Lamb, she is arrayed in "fine linen, bright and pure: for the fine linen is the righteous acts of the saints." Just as Paul looked forward to a consummation of the "marriage," so John looks forward to a consummation.

This raises the question as to when, in the thinking of John, the consummation of the marriage was to take place. It should be observed that the bride is the "wife" of the Lamb even before consummation of the marriage takes place. Such language is a reflection of the Jewish idea that a woman who was betrothed to a man was his wife; but, more than this, it is a symbol of the close union that always exists between Christ and his church. The church is always the bride of Christ in that he is her head and in that her life is pledged to him. But John speaks of the "marriage" of the Lamb, and Paul thought in terms of a more perfect union between Christ and his people. What is this more perfect union? It is the union of Christ and the redeemed that will be cemented beyond time and history following the overthrow of Satan, the resurrection, and the judgment. This is the consummation that will be effected when Christ returns in his second advent to claim his bride as his own.

Once again we must raise the question as to whether or not John predicted the end of the age and the Parousia, or the second advent, in his own time. Is the marriage of the Lamb a prediction of that which is imminent? Let us remember that, if we interpret this as a prophecy of that which is soon to take place, we must interpret almost all the prophecies of the book as having immediate fulfilment. We know that the prophecy concerning the fall of Rome was fulfilled, but not literally and not immediately. We shall face the same fact in connection with the appearance of Christ as King of kings and Lord of lords in 19:11–16, and in connection with the defeat of the beasts in 19:19–21. If we look forward to the vision of the New Jerusalem in chapter 21, we discover that the people of God are still the "bride, the wife of the Lamb," and this is as the New Jerusalem descends from heaven; that is to say, it takes place after the consummation of the age. To be sure, it is possible that the consummation of the marriage may be conceived of here as having taken place and that the "wife" remains a "bride" in marriage, but it would seem that this "coming down" of the New Jerusalem is in connection with the meeting with the Lamb for the marriage. However this may be, the author may be allowed in this vision to look forward, as he frequently does, to some future event and to present the event as if it were imminent or even accomplished. This was done, as we have seen, in the prediction of the fall of Rome. Now there is yet to be revealed by John the thousand-year reign of the saints in 20:1–4. This is a symbol, as we shall see, of a long period of time, undetermined in length. It is altogether likely that John had in mind the consummation of the "marriage" of the Lamb after the completion of the thousand years. The comment of Swete is pertinent on this point. He says: "It is the manner of the writer to throw out hints of the next great scene some time before he begins to enter upon it; thus, *Epesen epesen Babu-lōn* ('Fallen, fallen is Babylon') is heard in xiv. 8, though the fall itself does not come into sight before chapters xvii-xviii. Here in like manner the Marriage of the Lamb is announced as imminent (*ēlthen*), though a thousand years are yet to pass before its consummation (xx. 3), and the Bride is not revealed until we reach chapter xxi."[1] We conclude that the "marriage" of the Lamb is conceived of in the mind of John as certain but as being consummated at an undetermined time in the future.

The bride remains the "wife" of the Lamb. This in spite of the wooing of the beast that she forsake her betrothed. In contrast with the great harlot who gave herself willingly to the beast and who commits fornication with the kings of the earth, is the bride of the Lamb who refuses to accept the sinful invitation of the beast and maintains her purity. The harlot is "arrayed in purple and scarlet, and decked with gold and precious stone and pearls," but the bride of the Lamb is "clothed in fine linen, bright and pure," and "the fine linen is the righteous acts of the saints." The church, as the bride of the Lamb, is thus symbolized in her faithfulness to Christ by her resistance to emperor worship and to the Caesars. But, as the bride of Christ, she remains ever the expectant church who in purity and faithfulness waits for her betrothed to take her to himself.

Before this vision is done, John hears the command to write, and that which he must write is this: "Blessed are they that are bidden to the marriage supper of the Lamb." By the strange usages of apocalyptic imagery the "bride of the Lamb" must now become the guests at the wedding, for the bride is assuredly the people of God, and the guests at the marriage feast can only be the people of God. But this is no matter. Truth is truth under whatever symbol it may be given. When this command came to John, he fell down before the messenger to worship him but was restrained with the words: "See thou do it not: I am a fellow-servant with thee

[1]*Op. cit.*, p. 246.

179

and with thy brethren that hold the testimony of Jesus: worship God: for the testimony of Jesus is the spirit of prophecy." The one speaking to John is doubtless the angel of 17:1. But what is the meaning of his words?

The angel declares that he is a "fellow-servant with thee and with thy brethren that hold the testimony of Jesus." Who are those "that hold the testimony of Jesus"? They are those who preserve and carry on in the world the witness that he gave. He was the "faithful witness" who revealed God and God's kingdom over all; he was the "faithful witness" who sealed his testimony with his blood. Now those who "hold the testimony of Jesus" continue the witness that he began; they are those who bear testimony to the whole counsel of God as revealed in Jesus Christ, his life, his work, his teaching, his death, his resurrection, his exaltation to the right hand of God. Now it is this testimony that is "the spirit of prophecy." Those who are faithful to the testimony of Jesus are those who in the spirit of Jesus bear the testimony that he bore. It is this entering into the spirit of Jesus to bear the testimony that he gave that is "the spirit of prophecy." Jesus was the true prophet; he who is in the spirit of Jesus as a witness possesses the "spirit of prophecy." Because John had been faithful with his brethren in bearing the testimony of Jesus, he and they were counted worthy to be fellow servants with the angels. Such is the high appraisal placed upon faithful witnessing in the revelation that came to the Seer of Patmos.

Appearance of Christ for the Battle as King of Kings and Lord of Lords.—19:11–16

The great Captain of the hosts of God's army at last makes his appearance upon the stage. John says that he "saw the heaven opened; and behold, a white horse, and he that sat thereon called Faithful and True; and in righteousness he doth judge and make war." The marriage of the Lamb has been announced, and the bride has made herself ready, but this

180

one who comes forth from heaven is no bridegroom, nor is he a lamb; he is the warrior Captain of a host of fighting men. The white horse upon which he rides is a symbol of victory. This great warrior Captain is not to be confused with the rider who comes forth "conquering and to conquer" when the first seal of the scroll in the hand of God is opened by the Lamb. The first warrior is the symbol of earthly conquest; this warrior's name is "The Word of God." He is a warrior whose warfare is spiritual, for it is said "in righteousness he doth judge and make war." The weapon which he uses is spiritual, for we read, "And out of his mouth proceedeth a sharp sword, that with it he should smite the nations." This great warrior is none other than the Son of God, and he now appears for the battle against his enemies as King of kings and Lord of lords.

Can this be a representation of Christ in his Parousia, or second coming? This is possible, but if this be the interpretation that is given to the warrior Captain in his appearance here, it must follow that John conceived of the victory over the beasts which immediately follows as a supernatural victory. By now it should be clearly established that the beasts represent the imperial power and the priesthood of the emperor cult of John's own time. John is to picture these as being defeated in the battle with the warrior on the white horse. But no such defeat occurred in history as a supernatural event. There are interpreters who are not troubled about this. They claim that John prophesied the downfall of Rome and the defeat of the imperial power by Christ in his Parousia, but they freely admit that he erred in his prophecy. As we have heretofore suggested, such an error would not only cast doubt upon the validity of John's claim to inspiration, but it would also reveal him as a rather pathetic visionary whose view of history and of the purpose of God was quite limited and superficial. The dismissal of the problem with the assertion that John fell in with the common apocalyptic notions of the time is no solution. In his theology, in his interpretation of Christ and the gospel, in his fundamental

181

agreement with the great basic New Testament ideas, in his understanding of the ethical demands of the gospel, John is too great to be dismissed as one who was limited by the narrow Jewish apocalyptic eschatology which centered in the idea of the great victory of God over his enemies, to be won by a mighty supernatural act from heaven. Furthermore, if the author of the Revelation was limited by these narrow apocalyptic ideas, how was it that another great work originating in the province of Asia in the same period, the Gospel of John, gives no evidence that its author was limited by these narrow ideas? Now if the question be asked, Why, then, did John use the apocalyptic style if he did not believe in the apocalyptic interpretation of the gospel and history? the answer is that the apocalyptic style was admirably suited to his purpose. Not only did it provide a medium of symbolism that would shield the readers of the book from the charge of sedition, but it provided also an ideal literary form for the expression of the dramatic message he had to give. Beyond all this we should remember that John was writing in A.D. 95, or thereabouts, sixty-five years after Pentecost. It would seem that one writing at a time this far removed from the early days of the gospel would profit by the perspective that sixty-five years of the progress of Christianity would provide. It is strange that the interpreters of the "eschatological school" will not allow this. To these interpreters Jesus was an apocalyptist who looked for the coming of the kingdom of God by a mighty act of God's hand; the early Christians at Pentecost were apocalyptists who waited daily for the return of Jesus; Paul was dominated by the eschatological idea and constantly looked for the return of Christ in his own time; and of course the author of the Apocalypse was completely dominated by apocalyticism. Thus were all the great leaders dominated by a fundamental misconception of a movement which, in spite of this misapprehension of the character of the gospel by its chief protagonists, became the greatest creative force in the life of the world. It seems rather absurd to think that the men who knew Christianity best at its beginnings misunderstood it so sorely. Or are we to believe that they did not misunderstand it, that is to say, their understanding of Christianity was in keeping with the true character of Christianity? If this be the case, then we must admit that those who came after Jesus and Paul and John improved upon what Christianity was in the beginning, for certainly we must allow that this type of apocalyptic Christianity is inferior to that interpretation of Christianity which removes narrow apocalypticism from it. But here, lest we forget, according to the view of the men of the eschatological school themselves, there was that one exception to the early leaders who held apocalyptic views—the author of the Gospel of John, who, it is said, "spiritualized" the idea of the Parousia. Strangely enough, these interpreters do not reckon with the fact, as has been pointed out, that the Apocalypse originated in the same general locality in which the Fourth Gospel came to light and that it was written at approximately the same time; all of which should argue for the fact that the Seer of Patmos might well have employed apocalyptic imagery without being an apocalyptist in his interpretation of the gospel. Therefore, we say that, in his vision of the conquering Christ on the white horse, he is not picturing the supernatural appearance of Christ in his second advent to conquer his enemies, the beasts and their allies.

What, then, is symbolized by the warrior Captain on the white horse? The names of Christ in this vision and the figure of the sword proceeding from the mouth of the rider give a sufficient answer to the question. In the first place, "he hath a name written which no one knoweth but he himself." This is suggestive of the fact that there is a spiritual character about this personage which is incomprehensible to ordinary human beings. This implies the divine nature of Christ as Son of God. The character of Christ as Son of God is actually a great mystery which is to be accepted in faith by mortal men. When Peter confessed Jesus as "the Christ, the Son of the living God," he was told by Jesus, "Flesh and blood hath not revealed it unto thee, but my Father who is in heaven" (Matthew 16:16 f). Peter was able to confess Jesus as Son of God only by the aid of revelation. Such revelation is appropriated by means of the exercise of faith.

We are told further that the rider's name is called "The Word of God." This comes near to being the concept of Christ found in the Prologue of John's Gospel, Christ as the *Logos*, though we cannot be certain that the Seer of Patmos was employing the *Logos* concept here. There is no reason that he could not have employed it. In any event Christ is represented here as "The Word of God," by which it must certainly be meant that he is the utterance of God and the expression of the mind of God. By this name, then, Christ is presented as the perfect revelation of the will of God. As the perfect revealer of God's will and of God's thoughts, he comes to men to make known to them the truth of God that they may appropriate it and live it. Now this interpretation of this name of Christ finds emphasis in the figure of the sword which proceeds out of his mouth. It is with this sword that he makes war and is enabled to "smite the nations." Now all this teaches that Christ as warrior Captain is engaged in spiritual conquest. He is the Son of God who comes to men as a mystery, to be appropriated by faith; but he is also the Word of God who conquers by the revelation of God's truth and by the word of the gospel which proceeds as a sword from his mouth. Christ conquers, then, not by material warfare, but by winning of his way into the hearts of men who accept him in faith as the Son of God and by the dissemination of God's truth in the world. This is spiritual conquest. This is conquest by means of the winning of men to Christ and the gospel.

The other name of Christ in this vision is King of kings and Lord of lords. This name is the name that Christ won by virtue of the incarnation. It is not a new name received by him as he comes forth now as warrior Captain. Paul saw that Christ was King from the time he ascended to the right hand of God after the crucifixion and resurrection. In the great passage in Philippians in which Paul traces the descent of

184

THE GREAT DRAMA—ACT TWO

Christ from heaven to the cross and death, he declares that, as a result of this descent, "God highly exalted him, and gave unto him the name which is above every name; that in the name of Jesus every knee should bow, of things in heaven and things on earth and things under the earth, and that every tongue should confess that Jesus Christ is Lord, to the glory of God the Father" (Philippians 2:10 f). John has already referred to Christ in the very beginning of his book as "the ruler of the kings of the earth" (1:5). The great rule over the earth of God in Christ (11:15) is the very theme of the book. Thus this kingship of Christ indicated by the name King of kings and Lord of lords is not a kingship to be won in his victory over the beasts, or at his second advent; rather it is the kingship that belongs to him by virtue of his sojourn among men and his victory over death.

The Christ who comes forth for this great battle, therefore, appears to make spiritual warfare and to conquer by the power of the Word of God. The armies which follow him are from heaven. The members of these armies ride white horses, and in this they are seen to be victors, like their great Captain. But whereas they are "clothed in fine linen, white and pure," their leader is "arrayed in a garment sprinkled with blood." The blood on his garment is the symbol of the former conflicts through which he has passed. He "in the days of his flesh" fought and won hard battles with Satan and his hosts; the blood of these battles is still upon his garments; now he rides forth as a tested and tried leader to win yet other victories for God and the people of God. We are reminded here of the inspiring words of the author of the Epistle to the Hebrews: "Who in the days of his flesh, having offered up prayers and supplications with strong crying and tears unto him that was able to save him from death, and having been heard for his godly fear, though he was a Son, yet learned obedience by the things which he suffered; and having been made perfect, he became unto all them that obey him the author of eternal salvation" (Hebrews 5:7–9).

It was by the Word of God that Christ conquered the

185

Caesars; it is by the Word of God that he continues his conquest in history.

Invitation to the Great Supper of God and Defeat of the Beast and His Allies.—19:17–21

The great battle between the warrior Christ and his heavenly armies on the one side and the beast and his allies on the other is now at hand. This vision is begun with the appearance of an angel "standing in the sun" calling forth an invitation to "the birds that fly in mid heaven" to come to "the great supper of God." The prophet borrows in his vision from the imagery of Ezekiel, in his description of this gory feast of the "flesh of kings, and the flesh of captains, and the flesh of mighty men, and the flesh of horses and of them that sit thereon, and the flesh of all men, both free and bond, and small and great." The prototype of this feast (Ezekiel 39:17–20) pictures in dramatic if gory symbolism the triumph of Jehovah over the enemies of Israel in delivering Israel and "Jacob" (Ezekiel 39:25) from their captivity. The imagery in both the prophecy of Ezekiel and in Revelation is designed to picture the complete and terrible defeat of God's enemies; it provides the picture of a battlefield littered with dead bodies which have become food for the birds of carrion.

The battle is the battle of Har-Magedon foreseen in 16:16. Its quick termination is now described. John tells how he saw "the beast, and the kings of the earth, and their armies, gathered together to make war against him that sat upon the horse, and against his army. And the beast was taken, and with him the false prophet that wrought the signs in his sight, wherewith he deceived them that had received the mark of the beast and them that worshipped his image: they two were cast alive into the lake of fire that burneth with brimstone: and the rest were killed with the sword of him that sat upon the horse, even the sword which came forth out of his mouth: and all the birds were filled with their flesh."

This brief description of the defeat of the beast and his allies comes almost as an anticlimax in view of the emphasis heretofore placed upon the prospect of the event, and yet it is to the credit of the author that he does not indulge in an elaborate description of an imaginary battle. Such an elaborate description had been reserved for the prophecy of the destruction of Rome. This extended account of that event is fitting because of the dramatic contrast which Rome in her desolation offers to the New Jerusalem in her glory. The city of Rome served as a symbol of the whole imperial system; therefore, in the prophecy of Rome's doom, there was implied the collapse of the whole imperial system. Hence there is no demand for an extended description of the defeat of the beast here. The account given is eloquent in its brevity. The beast and the false prophet, by which is meant the priesthood of the emperor cult, are singled out in the vision for separate and distinct punishment. They are "cast alive into the lake of fire that burneth with brimstone." The followers of these two "are killed with the sword of him that sat upon the horse." It is quite natural that these two prominent characters in the drama should receive this separate treatment. The dire punishment of being cast alive into the "lake of fire," which is complete and utter defeat for the beasts, is in keeping with their prominence as leaders in the revolt of Satan against the rule of God in Christ. But it is the sword which came from the mouth of the warrior Captain that is the weapon of his conquest; it is with this sword that he slays the multitudes who followed the beast and the false prophet.

This is John's answer (though not his final answer) to the challenge by the Caesars to the rule of God in Christ. In apocalyptic imagery he has predicted that the imperial power will be utterly defeated in its attempt to force the churches to bow to the emperor as a god; in these strange symbols he has predicted the triumph of Christ and Christianity in the empire. Looking back on history, we know that there was no sudden destruction of the imperial power; we know that the emperors continued to reign for many years. But we do know

187

that in time the empire declined and fell. And we know also that Christianity survived the effort of Domitian and later emperors to suppress it. It was true that Christ won in this great conflict. He won by the power of the sword "which came forth out of his mouth," the sword of the implanted word of the gospel in human hearts and in society. The Word of God incarnate in Christ survived the wrath of the Caesars and brought victory to the cause of Christ in the world, a victory which extends even to our own time. It is by the Word of God incarnate in Christ that the gospel continues its onward victorious march in history.

The Binding of Satan.—20:1–3

Satan sustained his second great defeat in his failure to snatch the sovereignty over the world from Christ through his agents, the two beasts. His first great defeat came with his "fall from heaven" which followed the incarnation and the earthly work of Christ. The second defeat is now dramatized in the vision which describes Satan as being "bound" for a "thousand years." John gives his vision in these words: "And I saw an angel coming down out of heaven, having the key of the abyss and a great chain in his hand. And he laid hold on the dragon, the old serpent, which is the Devil and Satan, and bound him for a thousand years, and cast him into the abyss, and shut it, and sealed it over him, that he should deceive the nations no more, until the thousand years should be finished: after this he must be loosed for a little time."

Cast from heaven at his failure to destroy the Messiah, Satan is now cast from earth to the abyss, his rightful dwelling place. But this is not the end of his power; his final defeat is yet to come when he will be cast into "the lake of fire and brimstone" (20:10). Here is pictured the limitation of his power. The purpose of this limitation of his power is "that he should deceive the nations no more, until the thousand years should be finished."

What are we to understand as John's meaning by this use

of the figure of the "binding" of Satan? The earthly ministry of Jesus may provide the clue to its interpretation. We recall that when the seventy returned from their mission tour and reported that the demons were subject to them, Jesus cried out in exultation, "I beheld Satan fall as lightning from heaven" (Luke 10:18). The victory of Christ over the demons in his earthly ministry is thus seen to signalize that "fall" of Satan from heaven that John describes in Revelation 12:9. At another point in his ministry, Jesus was charged by the Pharisees with casting out demons by the power of Beelzebub, the prince of demons. In his reply Jesus declared that if "Satan casteth out Satan, he is divided against himself; how then shall his kingdom stand? . . . But if I by the Spirit of God cast out demons, then is the kingdom of God come upon you" (Matthew 12:26,28). This is followed by a parable: "Or how can one enter into the house of the strong *man*, and spoil his goods, except he first bind the strong *man*? And then he will spoil his house." The point of this parable is that Jesus is the Man stronger than the strong man, Satan, who is able to enter Satan's house, bind him, and spoil his goods. The parable is a representation of what Jesus was doing in invading Satan's realm to "bind" him and "spoil his goods"; that is, to cast out demons. Now this "binding" of Satan in the earthly ministry of Jesus is of the same character as that "binding" which John pictures here. The "binding" of Satan by Jesus in the casting out of demons prefigured that other "binding" that was to take place when Satan, the king of the abyss, which was the home of the demons (see Luke 8:31), was to suffer defeat at the hands of the exalted Christ in his effort to destroy the rule of God in Christ through the beast of imperial Rome. The purpose of this binding is to prevent Satan from deceiving the nations "until the thousand years should be finished." This harks back to the pouring out of the sixth bowl of wrath in 16:12–16. When this bowl was poured out, three unclean spirits came forth from the mouths of the dragon, the beast, and the false prophet. These are described as "spirits of demons, working signs; which go

189

forth unto the kings of the whole world to gather them together unto the war of the great day of God, the Almighty." These demons performed their work. John predicted that they would stir up the kings of the earth to resist God and attempt to overthrow his Christ in battle. He has prophesied the outcome of that conflict: Christ would be victorious. Now for a long period of time, undetermined in its duration, Satan, the king of the abyss and the demons (see 9:11), will be bound; that is, restrained in his power to deceive the nations as they had been deceived in attempting a battle of Armageddon against the reigning Christ.

Let it be repeated that this is not the termination of Satan's power; he has not been cast into the lake of fire; he is confined for a "thousand years" to the abyss, the home of the demons.

In the vision John teaches that with the failure of the Caesars to make Christianity subordinate to the imperial rule, the reign of Christ as King of kings and Lord of lords in history was confirmed. This reign is "one thousand years" in duration; that is, it is of a long period of time undetermined in duration. John prophesies that during this period it will not be possible for the nations to be deceived again as they were deceived in attempting to overthrow the reign of God in Christ. So far as the span of history which stretches from the triumph of Christianity in the first and second centuries to our own time is concerned, we may say that no instance is on record of a general challenge to the rule of Christ paralleling the challenge made to that rule by the empire of Rome, which ruled almost all the civilized world.

The Reign of the Martyrs and Saints, and the First Resurrection.—20:4–6

With the binding of Satan, there comes to John the vision of the reign of the martyrs and saints with Christ for a "thousand years." Let us permit the Seer to tell his vision in his own words:

And I saw thrones, and they sat upon them, . . . and *I
saw* the souls of them that had been beheaded for the testimony of Jesus, and for the word of God, and such as worshipped not the beast, neither his image, and received not the
mark upon their forehead and upon their hand; and they
lived, and reigned with Christ a thousand years. The rest of
the dead lived not until the thousand years should be finished. This is the first resurrection. Blessed and holy is he that
hath part in the first resurrection: over these the second
death hath no power; but they shall be priests of God and of
Christ, and shall reign with him a thousand years.

Before entering into a discussion of the meaning of this
controversial passage, it would be well for us to observe carefully what these words say and what they do not say. First
of all, it should be observed that they do *not* speak of the
reign of the martyrs and saints as being *upon the earth*. If
these words be construed as a prophecy of a millennial reign
upon the earth, such an interpretation cannot be based upon
any definite prediction here of such an earthly reign. John
states that he saw thrones; the implication is that these
thrones are occupied by the martyrs and saints, but whether
these thrones are in heaven or upon the earth, he does not
say. Heretofore John has had a vision of "thrones." Upon
these sat the four and twenty elders; assuredly the thrones
upon which they sat were in heaven (4:4). It is altogether
natural to think of these thrones upon which the martyrs and
saints sat as being in heaven.

In the second place, it should be observed that those who
occupy the thrones are not the martyrs only. Along with the
martyrs upon the thrones are "such as worshipped not the
beast, neither his image, and received not the mark upon
their forehead and upon their hand." This is a category which
is inclusive of all faithful Christians who lived in the era of
persecution under the Caesars. This description could certainly include the Christians who refused to surrender their
convictions during the reigns of both Nero and Domitian,
whether they were put to death or not; it includes all who

191

refused to receive the "mark of the beast," which would embrace all loyal Christians, in the reigns of these two emperors certainly. This fact should be remembered in the light of the view of some scholars that the book of Revelation has as one of its main objectives the glorification of martyrdom. This passage is interpreted by some as being in line with this view.

In the third place, it should be emphasized that this vision is related to a specific historical situation. These people who sit upon thrones and reign with Christ are people who had been "beheaded for the testimony of Jesus and for the word of God, and such as worshipped not the beast, neither his image, and received not the mark upon their forehead and upon their hand." This is, of course, an echo of 13:16 f and of 16:2, where mention is made of those who received the mark of the beast. John's vision is a prophecy of the reign with Christ of people who were faithful to Christ under the reign of those Caesars who persecuted the Christians and attempted to destroy Christianity; specifically, we can say, those who lived at the time of Nero and Domitian. It is a violation of the principles of historical exegesis, therefore, to make this vision applicable to saints who will reign with Christ in some earthly kingdom yet to be. It is quite proper to apply spiritually the prophecy here made to all the saints through the ages who are faithful to Christ. But when such interpretation is made, let it be understood that the prophecy is being applied in principle and not literally.

Continuing our scrutiny of the words of the passage before us, it is to be observed that a distinction is made between those who occupy thrones and reign with Christ and "the rest of the dead." Who are the "rest of the dead"? If, as the words of the vision plainly state, those who reign with Christ the thousand years are all faithful Christians living at the time of Domitian (and including those who suffered martyrdom or were faithful in Nero's persecution), the "rest of the dead" might apply to either or both of two groups: (1) all other Christians of other times who had no occasion to resist persecution; (2) all non-Christians. The view is taken here that the "rest of the dead" refers to all non-Christians, though the reference may be specifically to those who received the mark of the beast, by way of contrasting their state with those who refused the mark of the beast. The basis for interpreting the "rest of the dead" in this way is the statement that follows: "This is the first resurrection. Blessed and holy is he that hath part in the first resurrection: over these the second death hath no power." If the "rest of the dead" is to refer to Christians as well as non-Christians, then we must admit that John visualizes a "special" resurrection for a favored class and at the same time implies that hosts of Christians who did not live in a time of persecution are to be exposed to the "second death." Now from 20:14 we learn that the "second death" is "the lake of fire" into which Satan is to be cast for his final defeat. It is difficult to believe that John meant to teach either a special "first" resurrection for a favored class of Christians, or that Christians who did not live in a time of persecution were to be numbered among "the rest of the dead," all of whom would be exposed to the "second death." It is more reasonable to take "the rest of the dead" as applying to those who received the mark of the beast and died without accepting the sovereignty of God in Christ. In principle the category might be used in reference to all who die without Christ, for it is reasonable to think that the fate of those who reject Christ in any age ultimately will be the same fate of those who died with the mark of the beast upon them.

Now, therefore, a word may be said concerning the "first" resurrection. The "first" resurrection as seen in this vision is that resurrection which occurred when the souls of the saints who died arose to be with Christ. This resurrection is similar to the resurrection of each saint who dies; it is the resurrection of the spirit which takes place in the case of every faithful believer when his soul departs from the body to be with Christ. This resurrection is to be distinguished from the "general" resurrection which John is to see in the vision of the multitudes "standing before the throne" to be judged out of the books that were opened (20:12). The probability that this is the proper interpretation to be placed upon the "first" resurrection is strengthened by the meaning of the Greek aorists that are used here. "They lived (*ezēsa,* ingressive aorist) and reigned with Christ, etc.", may well be translated "they *came alive* and reigned with Christ, etc." "The rest of the dead lived (*ezēsa,* ingressive aorist) not until the thousand years should be finished," may be better rendered, "The rest of the dead did not *come alive, etc.*" This is not to be construed as a doctrine of "dreamless sleep" or "suspended animation" for the wicked dead. It is only to say that the "rest of the dead" will not have the privilege of arising from death to share the life of Christ and his blessed saints in the thousand-year reign.

We should now take notice of the Old Testament background of the passage and its significance for the meaning of the vision. The "thrones" and the reference to the risen saints as "priests of God and of Christ" who will reign with him a thousand years indicate that the passage has as its background the visions of Daniel in Daniel 7. (The passage also echoes the words of Jehovah in Exodus 19:6). We have shown that the great proclamation of the sovereignty of God in Christ in Revelation 11:15 is closely related to the vision of the everlasting dominion given to "one like unto a son of man" in Daniel 7:13-14. Further along in this chapter Daniel receives an interpretation of this vision. Among the matters explained to him is that "the saints of the Most High shall receive the kingdom, and possess the kingdom for ever, even for ever and ever. . . . and judgment was given to the saints of the Most High, and the time came that the saints possessed the kingdom" (Daniel 7:18,22). As has been shown, this "everlasting kingdom" in Daniel was interpreted as referring to the reign of the Messiah. The early Christians, as we have seen, interpreted the messianic reign as having begun with the resurrection of Jesus. This line of evidence points strongly to the fact that this vision of the reign of the martyrs and saints in Revelation is another vision of the messianic reign. The Messiah has arisen from the dead to sit upon his throne; now the "saints of the Most High," experiencing the "first" resurrection, "possess the kingdom," occupying thrones and reigning jointly with the Messiah. If this be the correct view, the one thousand years is a symbol of the messianic reign. In the light of what we know concerning the view of the early Christian teachers as to the time of the beginning of the Messiah's reign, we are safe in saying that this one-thousand-year period is conceived of as having its beginning with the establishment of Christ as Messiah at the right hand of God. Furthermore, it may be emphasized that, in primitive Christian thought, the messianic reign was a spiritual reign and was by no means conceived of as a temporal reign of Christ upon the earth.

These things being so, we may conclude that, in this vision of the millennium in Revelation 20:4–6, the thousand-year reign is thought of as the spiritual reign of Jesus Christ and his saints which began with his exaltation to the right hand of God and which will continue until the end of history.

With respect to the length of the thousand years, there is no warrant for taking this figure literally. The other numbers designating periods of time in Revelation are symbols. In 11:2 the "forty and two months" (three and a half years) symbolizes a limited period of war and persecution; the "one hour" of 17:12 is symbolic of the very brief time that the ten kings reign with the beast. All these numbers indicating periods of time connected with the persecution of Christians or with the reign of evil world powers are symbols of periods of time short in duration. By way of contrast with these, the messianic reign is almost eternal—it is one thousand years in duration! That the thousand years here is a symbol of a long period of time, undetermined in duration, receives support from the statement in 2 Peter 3:8: "But forget not this one thing, beloved, that one day is with the Lord as a thousand years, and a thousand years as one day."

This symbolism of the thousand years has its parallel in the apocalyptic literature. *The Book of the Secrets of Enoch,* which is dated by R. H. Charles in the period A.D. 1–50, conceives of the days of creation in Genesis as being of one thousand years each in duration and presents a scheme of world history seven thousand years in duration. According to this scheme, the cycle of creation was seven days; that is, seven thousand years. After this cycle God created an eighth day to begin a new cycle of seven thousand years. When this seven-thousand-year cycle is completed, there is to be an eighth day, concerning which it is said, "And that at the beginning of the eighth thousand there should be a time of not-counting, endless, with neither years nor months nor weeks nor days nor hours."[2] This last day of a thousand years is obviously intended to represent eternity: it is a time of "not-counting." Nothing is said in this passage as to the seventh thousand-year period's being the messianic era, but this is implied. This seventh thousand years is the last era of history, and it is followed by eternity. (Eternity follows the one thousand years in Revelation.) Also, the seventh thousand years corresponds with the seventh day of the first cycle in which God rested from his creation. There is in this the implication that the second seventh thousand-year period will be a period of rest and peace; that is, the messianic age.

The materialistic interpretation of the millennium in Revelation, that is, that interpretation which makes of the thousand years an actual physical reign of Christ upon the earth, is first found in Christian thought in the writings of Papias, the church father who died by martyrdom about A.D. 163, and who claimed to have known individuals who knew John and others of the apostles. Eusebius, the church historian, records the fact that Papias said "that there will be a millennium after the resurrection from the dead, when the personal reign of Christ will be established upon this earth."[3] It is highly significant that Papias derives his conception of the

[2]The Book of the Secrets of Enoch, 33:2, quoted from The Apocrypha and Pseudepigrapha of the Old Testament, Vol. II, by R. H. Charles, p. 451.

[3]Ecclesiastical History, iii. 39, quoted from Ante-Nicene Christian Library, edited by Roberts and Donaldson, Edinburgh: T. and T. Clark, Vol. I, p. 445.

character of the millennium from a non-canonical apocalyptic work, *Second Baruch;* although he seems to attribute
this teaching to Jesus himself. Irenaeus, the church father
(*Against Heresies*, v. 32), quotes Papias in the following
manner:

> [As the elders who saw John the disciple of the Lord re-
> membered that they had heard from him how the Lord
> taught in regard to those times, and said]: "The days will
> come in which vines shall grow, having ten thousand branches,
> and in each branch ten thousand twigs, and in each true
> twig ten thousand shoots, and in every one of the shoots ten
> thousand clusters, and on every one of the clusters ten thou-
> sand grapes, and every grape when pressed will give five-
> and-twenty metretes of wine."[4]

Papias goes on to say that Judas the traitor was skeptical
about these predictions and asked how such things could
come to pass. Jesus is said to have replied, "They shall see
who shall come to them." Papias then concludes with this
comment: "These, then, are the times mentioned by the
prophet Isaiah: 'And, the wolf shall lie down with the lamb,'
etc. (Isa. xi. 6 ff.)."[5]

To discover the source of Papias' ideas concerning the messianic age, it is only necessary to read from the apocalyptic
work, *Second Baruch*, 29: 5,6: "The earth also shall yield its
fruit ten thousandfold and on each (?) vine there shall be
a thousand branches, and each branch shall produce a thousand clusters, and each cluster produce a thousand grapes
and each grape produce a cor of wine."[6] Charles dates this
work in the period A.D. 50–90.

This examination of the statements of Papias sheds interesting light upon the problem of the source of the materialistic conception of the millennium. Papias attributes to Jesus

[4]*Ibid.*

[5]*Ibid.*, p. 443.

[6]Quoted from *Apocrypha and Pseudepigrapha of the Old Testament*, by
R. H. Charles, Vol. II, p. 497 f.

words which he never uttered and derives his notion of the messianic age from an apocalyptic work. Apparently Papias did not square his notions with the concept of the millennium in the book of Revelation, or else he misinterpreted what he found there, for he places the millennium after the resurrection. (See the quotation from Eusebius' *Ecclesiastical History*, iii. 39 above.) In Revelation the general resurrection comes after the thousand years (20:12). It is possible, of course, that Papias interpreted the "first resurrection" of 20:6 as the general resurrection. If this be the case, then Papias interpreted the one thousand years of Revelation 20:4 as the time "when the personal reign of Christ will be established upon this earth." It is altogether possible that in Papias we have discovered the source of all later materialistic interpretation of the millennium in Christian thought.

Swete has some interesting comments on the interpretation of the millennium in early Christian thought.[7] Commenting on Dr. Charles' view that John in Revelation was thinking in terms of an earthly millennium [*Eschatology*, 2nd Ed., p. 407], he uses Justin Martyr as an illustration of how "early Christian interpretation fell into the same snare." He goes on to say: "There were, however, even in Justin's days many Christians who refused to accept the chiliastic interpretation of St. John's vision, as Justin himself candidly confesses. At Alexandria in the third century a materialistic chiliasm was strongly condemned by Origen, and Dionysius." Dr. Swete states further: "To Augustine the Church owes the first serious effort to interpret Apoc. xx (*de civ. Dei* xx. 7 ff.). He confesses that he at one time had been disposed to adopt a modified chiliasm, in which 'deliciae spirituales' were substituted for the sensuous expectations of the early *milliarii*. But a longer study of the subject led him to a different conclusion. He had learned to see in the captivity of Satan nothing else than the binding of the strong man by the Stronger than he which the Lord had foretold (Mc. iii. 27, Lc. xi. 22); in the thousand years, the whole interval between the first

[7] *The Apocalypse of St. John*, p. 265 f.

Advent and the last conflict; in the reign of the Saints, the entire course of the Kingdom of Heaven; in the judgment given to them, the binding and loosing of sinners; in the first resurrection, the spiritual share in the Resurrection of Christ which belongs to the baptized (Col. iii. 1). This exegesis finds a place in most of the ancient commentators, both Greek and Latin, who wrote after Augustine's time." Because of its pertinence and clarity, we may add Dr. Swete's comment:

> There are points at which the Augustinian interpretation forsakes the guidance of St. John's words; it overlooks, e.g., the limitation of the first Resurrection to the martyrs and confessors. But on the whole it seems to be on right lines. The symbolism of the Book is opposed to a literal understanding of the Thousand Years, and of the resurrection and reign of the Saints with Christ. It is "the souls" of the martyrs that St. John sees alive; the resurrection is clearly spiritual and not corporeal. Augustine's reference to the parable of the Strong Man armed is illuminating in a high degree, even if it is impossible to press it to the precise conclusion which he reached.

By way of conclusion, what shall we say of a practical nature? Again let it be emphasized that John visualized in Revelation 20:4-6 no physical reign of Christ and his saints upon the earth. The one thousand years is a symbol of the messianic reign, and as such is to be conceived of as beginning when Christ completed his work upon earth and ascended to the right hand of God. The messianic reign, in so far as history is concerned, is to be terminated with the end of history; the one thousand years extend, therefore, to the consummation of the age and the second advent of the Lord. This is not to say that the reign of Christ will terminate with the consummation of the age, but that his reign over human history will terminate because history is no longer existent. However, Christ is the King-Messiah who will reign with God for ever and ever, and with God and Christ the redeemed will reign through all eternity. But Christ is King of kings and Lord of lords *now* and, as such, reigns from the right hand of God. John conceived of that reign, in so far as human history is concerned, as continuing one thousand years. We who live today, therefore, are in the millennium.

The Final Defeat of Satan.—20:7–10

John looks now toward the end of history. The Seer has seen in his vision a long course in history for the reign of God in Christ, but he has seen no complete overthrow of Satan. The power of Satan was to be limited—he was to be "bound" for the "thousand" years of the messianic reign, but there was to be no final defeat for the dragon who had inspired the beast, until the end of time. John has shown both restraint and the wisdom of a true prophet in this outlook upon the whole course of history in its relation to the events of his own time. He has had much to say concerning the events of his own time; these he has treated in great detail. By way of contrast he will have little to say concerning the end of history. His account of the happenings at the end is starkly brief; to those who are inspired by curiosity concerning the happenings of the last days, his summary treatment of the final defeat of Satan is disappointing. With one brief sentence he dismisses the whole vast cataclysm of the end. It is: "And fire came down out of heaven, and devoured them." This, and this only, after the lurid details of Rome's burning! This, and only this, after the visions of the bowls of wrath! But herein does John reveal the proper reserve and the wisdom of a true prophet. That there would be an end of time, the Seer of Patmos knew full well; that history must have its consummation in the complete victory of Christ over Satan, John firmly believed; but the manner of this victory and the time of its coming he was content to leave veiled in the mists of the future and in the counsels of God. John was content to let one brief sentence serve as the recital of the story of the actual end: "Fire came down out of heaven, and devoured them." That would say that the end would come; that would say that God brought the end; that would say that the enemies of God were forever conquered; this, then, was enough. How strange it is, therefore, that men have taken his book to be almost exclusively a scheme of the things that are to take place at the end!)

But let us say that John is a wise prophet again in that, while he has no lurid description to give of events to transpire at the consummation of history, he does reckon with the end. He could not be the true prophet unless this were so. John keeps his perspective by thus holding the end always in view. If Satan could only be "bound" during the messianic reign, nevertheless he would be destroyed in the end. And there was beyond the end of history the New Jerusalem, the City of God! Only he who reckons with the consummation of history is capable of affirming the New Jerusalem. Now John was forced to behold in the actualities of history in his own day Babylon, the wicked city of earth. This metropolis of iniquity he looked upon as the great harlot of the earth. But even as he was forced to look upon the wicked city of earth and see her as the harlot, his spirit's eye could look beyond the end to the New Jerusalem as the bride of Christ. The harlot he was compelled to look upon; the bride he rejoiced to see with the eye of faith!

This capacity of the prophet to keep the end in view, to interpret the present in the light of the consummation, is sorely needed in our own time. Modern Christianity needs the depth and stability that such a wholesome eschatological outlook gives. We have lost in much of our preaching and interpretation of the gospel the sense of God's hand in history, of his direction of history toward a goal and consummation. We need the validation of our doctrine in a robust certainty that there is a consummation that God is bringing to pass. What are love and justice and peace and morality apart from the conviction that these are supported by the eternal purposes of God in history? And how shall we decry sin and fight against evil unless we know that God will completely vindicate his holiness in a final judgment? And how shall we comfort our broken hearts and help heal the wounds of humanity unless there is a new heaven and a new earth and a New Jerusalem wherein there is "a river of water of life"? Yes, we do need this wholesome sense of the end which the Seer of Patmos had!

Likewise we need the wholesome realism displayed by John in his interpretation of the sovereignty of God in Christ in the world. In his vision of the binding of Satan, he saw that Satan would be "bound" but not destroyed; he saw that he would be cast into the "abyss" but not into "the lake of fire"; he saw that there would come a time when "he must be loosed for a little time." And all the while John saw Christ reigning as King of kings and Lord of lords from the right hand of God. This is to say that John could affirm the sovereignty of God in Christ and at the same time allow for the presence of evil in the world. As we have said, John believed in no perfect order in society; he was too much of a realist and too much of a true prophet to fall into the error of interpreting the kingdom of God as a perfect order in society. He saw there could be no perfect order this side of eternity. And yet he believed passionately in the reign of God in Christ. Likewise, with all his consciousness of the end of history, he vigorously asserted the great ethical imperatives of the gospel. His watchword to the erring churches of Asia was "Repent!" Certainly, then, he must have believed in progress in history and in the development of a good society; but he never fell into the error of superficial modern interpreters of the kingdom of God who equate the kingdom with a perfect society or think of it as arising out of history through an evolutionary process. John conceived of the kingdom as NOW, and as the sovereignty of God operative in history in the person and work of Jesus Christ, as God's rule over men on the basis of the revelation of himself made in Jesus of Nazareth. But that such a rule would produce finally through a process of evolution a perfect order in society was no thought of John's. Progress there would be, yes; and increasing enlightenment, and a developing conscience inspired by the teaching and spirit of Jesus; but a perfect social order, no.

It was the wisdom of the true prophet in John that led him, then, to allow for a final conflict between Christ and Satan on the plane of history. He clothes his brief statement concerning this conflict in the usual apocalyptic imagery. Satan was to be "loosed out of his prison" after the thousand years were finished. Once more he would "come forth to deceive the nations" as he had deceived them through the beast of imperial Rome. The nations are symbolized under Ezekiel's mystical names, "Gog and Magog" (see Ezekiel 38–39). Perhaps the names originally applied to the terrible Scythian invaders; to John the names are mere symbols of the fierce enemies of Christ and the people of God in this last battle. At last they make the great attack upon the people of God: they "compassed the camp of the saints about, and the beloved city." The "camp of the saints" and the "beloved city" are simply symbols of all the people of God living upon the earth when the final assault of Satan is made. God brings the end and the victory. There is no suggestion that the saints lift a hand in defense; it is simply said that "fire came down out of heaven, and devoured them." This is God's doing, not man's; the victory is from heaven, not of earth.

And now comes the utter and complete defeat of Satan. "And the devil that deceived them was cast into the lake of fire and brimstone, where was also the beast and the false prophet; and they shall be tormented day and night for ever and ever."

It is not for us to attempt to go beyond what the prophet has given us here as to the nature of the end. To do that would be to attempt to pry into mysteries that are hid from mortal eyes and that are locked in the counsels of God. It becomes us to be as reserved and as chaste as was John in his account of the end. As to how the consummation will be effected, it is only given us to know that God will bring it to pass; as to when the end will come, it is enough for us to know that it will be "when the thousand years are finished"; as for "times and seasons," it is for us who obey the Word of the Lord to be content not to know them.

Scene Seven

THE JUDGMENT, THE NEW HEAVEN AND THE NEW EARTH, AND THE NEW JERUSALEM

(Chapters 20:11 to 22:5)

WE now pierce the veil of eternity with the Seer of Patmos. In so far as his drama pertains to the earthly course of events, it is done. Satan has been consigned forever to the lake of fire; the Almighty has rung down the curtain upon human history; there remains but the brief vision of that event in eternity in which all men who have lived pause to catch the last directive of the Great Judge, and beyond this the final vision glorious of the life everlasting.

The Resurrection, the Judgment, and the End of Death.—20:11–15

The earth and the heaven have "fled away" in this vision to leave in view "a great white throne." There is no description of the one who sits upon this throne, but we can sense the awesome majesty of his presence and we know he is the Almighty. Before him as the Great Judge stand "the dead, the great and the small." The sea had given up its dead, and death and Hades had given up their dead in order that they, too, might stand before the great throne. This is the general resurrection. There is no mention of its having taken place, but the vision is of all men who ever lived standing before the throne. Even those who had lost their lives at sea, whose resting place in death had never been seen or marked—these are brought living before the great throne. The great and the small are there—it is the final gathering of all souls who ever drew the breath of life, before the last separation of the righteous and the wicked is made. "Death and Hades" had given up their dead. These represent, as Swete points out, "the two aspects of Death, the physical fact and its spiritual consequences. . . . Here they appear as two voracious and insatiable monsters who have swallowed all past generations, but are now forced to disgorge their prey."[1] Only the final resurrection makes such a gathering possible. This is the resurrection which stands in contrast with the "first resurrection" of 20:5-6.

"Books were opened: and another book was opened" before the great white throne. The "books" are those that contain the records of the works of all those who stand before the great Judge. The "book" is the "book of life." In it are written the names of all the redeemed of all time. And "they were judged every man according to their works. . . . And if any man was not found written in the book of life, he was cast into the lake of fire."

Here then, pictorially conceived, are *the great realities* of the final judgment, of the general resurrection, of the ultimate separation of good and evil, of the condemnation of the wicked, of the final reward of the righteous. However these great spiritual realities may be presented to the human understanding, they are true. John believed them and incorporated them in his drama because they belonged to the body of Christian teaching received by him. Jesus taught these realities—every one of them. They belonged to that dynamic eschatology that infused all his teaching and that gave the validity of eternity to his ethical system. Without them his teaching would not be his teaching; without them the gospel is an attenuated gospel; without them there is no complete statement of Christian doctrine. To the mortal minds that

[1]*Op. cit.,* p. 273.

205

must grasp his message, John brings these great realities in symbols; they are none the less real for being in symbols. To the persecuted saints of his own day this vision of the judgment would come as an assurance that God was just; to the wavering saint it would come as a warning that lukewarm service to Christ was unacceptable; to all it would serve as an assurance that there was a destiny for even the least of God's children, for it was said that "the great and the small" would arise from the dead to stand before the throne of judgment.

Last of all, death was to be forever abolished. "And death and Hades were cast into the lake of fire." The great apostle Paul had said, "The last enemy that shall be abolished is death" (1 Corinthians 15:26). John is true in his vision to this teaching. This must be true if God is and if Christ lives! Death cannot forever exist if God is to reign, for eternal death would be a denial of the *living* God. Death must die if eternal life is to be real; death must die if the gateway to the New Jerusalem is to open! The faithful Christians of John's day, who had seen their loved ones led off to die because of their loyalty to Christ, would rejoice in this assurance that the last enemy would be conquered; the martyrs themselves, as they "lifted white brows to the sky," would die with songs of praises on their lips when these words echoed in their ears. And all the long line of those who loved the Lord from that day until this have gladly received those words that "death and Hades were cast into the lake of fire." With the apostle Paul they have said, in the knowledge of that certainty, "O death, where is thy victory? O death, where is thy sting? . . . thanks be to God, who giveth us the victory through our Lord Jesus Christ."

Introduction to the Coming Age.—21:1–8

Beyond the judgment is the City of God, the New Jerusalem. But before we are given a view of the celestial city in all its glories, we shall see in the vision of John the wonders of the coming age and hear a recital of the blessings that are reserved in eternity for the people of God. There is introduction here of the New Jerusalem, but we must wait for a more elaborate description of the dwelling place of the redeemed. Our author is now concerned with an attempt to give expression to the indescribable glory of the *experience* of life everlasting with God.

It is "a new heaven and a new earth," by which the author means this age is a new creation, having no elements of the old physical earth and sky in it. The heaven here cannot refer to the heaven which is the dwelling place of God and the angels; rather it is that portion of the cosmos which lay above and around the earth, perhaps the "dome of the sky" with its multitude of stars. It may well represent the whole physical cosmos outside the earth. This in the author's mind is doubtless a fulfilment of Isaiah's prophecy: "For, behold I create new heavens, and a new earth; and the former things shall not be remembered, nor come into mind" (Isaiah 65:17). This is the new cosmos, the new order of things concerning which prophets and wise men have spoken for centuries. Such a new creation was looked for by the Stoic philosophers who believed that a renovation of the world was a necessary reality of the future. John sees that the "new Jerusalem, coming down out of heaven from God, made ready as a bride, adorned for her husband," belonged to this new creation. The characteristic of this creation that contrasts it so sharply with the old order is that it is *new*. In his vision of the judgment, John saw that "the earth and the heaven" had fled away from the face of him who sat upon the throne; there was no place for the old; its course had been run. With the old physical order dissolved, we stand in the midst of a cosmos that is *purely spiritual,* unbounded by earth and sky, unrestrained by flesh and blood, unhampered by human emotions and bodily senses. "And he that sitteth on the throne said, Behold, I make all things new." This is the ultimate experience of the people of God, the goal of all spiritual life, the end of all righteousness, the consummation of all dreams of complete mastery of sin and self. This is the heaven that is to be beyond death, beyond resurrection, beyond judgment.

The central dynamic of this suprahistorical experience is the glorious presence of the *eternal* God. "Behold, the tabernacle of God is with men, and he shall dwell with them, and they shall be his peoples, and God himself shall be with them." The beautiful picture reflects the experience of the Israelites as they marched toward the Promised Land. The center of their life in their desert wanderings was the Tabernacle. It was here that Jehovah dwelt; it was here that he shed his *shekinah* (presence). The people saw his manifestation in the pillar of cloud by day and the pillar of fire by night. By these tokens they knew that Jehovah was in their midst. But this was a mere figure of the experience reserved for the people of God in the new age. In that age which John sees in his vision, God will be forever with his people, "he shall dwell with them," or, better, as the Greek has it, "he shall pitch his tent with them" (*skenōsei*). So near will the Almighty be to his people in this experience beyond time and space that it may be said that his tent will be among the tents of those who are his people.

This experience beyond history will have no place in it for suffering. Here will be found the final victory over all pain, all sorrow. God's presence will assure this victory over earth's defeats. He "shall wipe away every tear from their eyes; and death shall be no more; neither shall there be mourning, nor crying, nor pain, any more: the first things are passed away." These are blessed and precious words to all God's people who in passing through "this vale of tears" have known the meaning of a broken heart. They comforted and inspired the persecuted and brokenhearted of John's day; they have comforted and inspired millions who since their day have known the pangs of heartbreak and sorrow. They have a meaning for every saint of God who knows or will know the cruel ways of suffering and the dark days of death. Those who know that beyond this sphere of mortal weakness there lies the heavenly experience of victory over suffering and death, can and do take hold of life here and live it victoriously in spite of the tears and the heartbreaks it brings.

The assurance of the vision is that all the blessings of the new age are freely given. "I will give unto him that is athirst of the fountain of water of life freely." But these marvelous blessings are reserved for those only who have proved their right to them. "He that overcometh shall inherit these things; and I will be his God, and he shall be my son." Now John displays again his belief in the great ethical imperatives of the gospel. He will not speak of the heavenly experience and imply that this heavenly experience is cheaply bought. He will not give a distorted view of the gospel of Christ which makes of it an other-worldly affair that has little relation to the everyday lives and affairs of men. He will not fall into the error of some who separate eschatology from ethics, or make a chasm between morals and religion. He knows that in the gospel of Jesus Christ all life is comprehended, and that orthodoxy in doctrine demands orthodoxy in living. He will not forget, in his flight into the realm of the mystical elements of our religion, that there is a practical side of that life which demands holy living. For those who talk glibly of heaven and their assurance of going there, for those who interpret Christianity as a religion of the other world only, John has this highly important warning:

> But for the fearful, and unbelieving, and abominable, and murderers, and fornicators, and sorcerers, and idolaters, and all liars, their part shall be in the lake that burneth with fire and brimstone; which is the second death.

Appearing as they do in the midst of glowing descriptions of the glories and wonders of the new age, these words come as a sudden shock, striking the consciousness like the darts of sharp arrows and rudely awakening the reader from his enjoyment of his flight with the Seer into the world to come. They bring us back sharply to the present order of workaday life and compel us to face the stern, ethical imperatives of our faith. They demand that we ask ourselves the questions:

Are we living the life of the redeemed? Are we presuming upon our salvation? Are we assuring ourselves that, since we believe right, all is well with our souls? Are we dealing superficially with sin? Are we placing the whole burden of victory over sin upon Christ? Have we forgotten that there is a cross for each one of us too? Are we thinking of Christian experience as acceptance of a creed rather than union with Jesus Christ? Are we substituting activity in the church for service in the world? Have we relegated the commandments of the man Jesus to a place of secondary importance? These unpleasant words of the Seer about fornicators, idolaters, liars, and other transgressors of the laws of God, appearing in the midst of glowing words about the life to come, should serve to remind us that there is a definite relationship between the life to come and the life that now is. We are to live in the light of this fact. We move toward the coming age with each passing day of our earthly lives. As to that age John reminds us of God's promise that he will dwell with us and that to each one personally and individually he will be Father: "and I will be his God, and he shall be my son." In this promise is the assurance that every life lived upon the planet may have eternal significance. The destiny of every human being, however unimportant, is to be a son of God! In the challenge of that destiny, each child of God upon the earth should see his life invested with the glory of eternity and divine sonship; and, seeing it so invested, he should lead the life worthy of him who is to live forever with God as a son of God.

The New Jerusalem: the Perfect City.—21:9 to 22:5

The New Jerusalem now comes clearly into sight. She stands in marked contrast with Babylon, the wicked city of earth, which has perished. The author had viewed Babylon when carried away in the Spirit "in a wilderness"; he is carried by the Spirit "to a mountain great and high" to see the New Jerusalem. The old city is a harlot, the consort of the beast; the new city is the bride, the wife of the Lamb. The

210

city of earth is now the city of death; the heavenly city is the city of life in which is to be found the river of water of life, and the tree of life with its leaves "for the healing of the nations." Babylon was the sinful, imperfect city; the New Jerusalem is the holy, perfect city. The old city had arisen from the earth; the new city comes down "out of heaven."

This is indeed the City of God; it is God's creation, not man's. It is no picture of that which arises by an evolutionary process out of history; it is a picture of that which comes down from God. Therefore, we have in this vision an incomparable representation of the redeemed of God of all time in the life of the Spirit that they are to live beyond time and space. It is idle to attempt to use the symbols of this majestic poem to unlock the mysteries of heaven and display to mortal minds the secrets of life beyond the grave. This grand poem is no philosophic treatise on immortality; it tells more about heaven than any such treatise could possibly tell. But we shall miss the mark if we attempt to press the symbolism to provide for us an understandable picture of heaven. The author did not intend to give us an exact picture of heaven as a place. He employs language and symbols in rich variety to present as well as language can present them the great spiritual truths about heaven and the life everlasting. We shall do well to keep in mind that John is thinking in terms of the great *spiritual experience* to which the people of God are destined, and is attempting as best he may to reveal the glories of that experience in language that must be couched in symbols suggestive of tangible objects, time, and space.

The New Jerusalem is "the bride, the wife of the Lamb." The implication is that the marriage of the Lamb promised in 19:7 has now taken place, for in 21:2 the city is pictured as "made ready as a bride adorned for her husband." The "thousand years" of 20:4–5 are over, Satan has been cast into "the lake of fire and brimstone" to remain in this place of torment forever, history has been brought to its end, and the redeemed of all the ages are now united in indivisible union with the Lamb. Christ has claimed his bride, the marriage

211

has been consummated, Christ and his church are one. Thus we may say that the Parousia, or the second advent, has taken place. How or at what point this great event transpired, John does not say. Perhaps he has deliberately obscured this great coming of Christ to claim his bride in order not to be presumptuous in the fixing of "times and seasons." Perhaps his reserve was dictated by the words of the Lord: "But of that day and hour knoweth no one, not even the angels of heaven, neither the Son, but the Father only" (Matthew 24:36).

We may profit by the great spiritual lessons John's glowing picture of the New Jerusalem teaches us. An analysis of the passage shows that there are seven outstanding characteristics of the heavenly city. Babylon, the wicked city of earth, was condemned seven times over; the New Jerusalem, the City of God, is praised for her seven matchless virtues.

1. *The New Jerusalem is perfect in her glory.*—Using the sacred number 12, John repeats it seven times to indicate the utter perfection of the heavenly city. The city is described as "having the glory of God." And now see how John reveals her glory: (1) The city has 12 gates; (2) there are 12 angels at the gates; (3) the names of 12 tribes are on the gates; (4) there are 12 foundations to the wall of the city; (5) the names of the 12 apostles of the Lamb appear on the foundation; (6) the city is a perfect cube, 12 by 12 by 12 thousand furlongs in its dimensions (a furlong is approximately 660 feet)—this feature being suggestive of the Holy of holies of the Temple, a perfect cube; (7) the wall of the city is 12 by 12 cubits. To add to this suggestion of perfection, the author describes the city as having light like that which flashed from a jasper stone, "clear as crystal"; as having its wall constructed of jasper; as being built throughout of pure gold; as having walls whose foundations are of precious stones; as having gates made of pearls, each gate being itself a pearl; and of having streets that are made of pure gold.

2. *The New Jerusalem is a city of perfect worship.*—John says he "saw no temple therein: for the Lord God the Al-

mighty, and the Lamb, are the temple thereof." The presence of God and of the Lamb with the redeemed renders worship in temples unnecessary. To be in the presence of God and the Lamb is to worship. The whole heavenly experience is to be an experience of continuous worship.

3. *The New Jerusalem is perfect in its universality.*—It is the city of perfect refuge for all people of all races and nations. "And the nations shall walk amidst the light thereof: and the kings of the earth bring their glory into it. And the gates thereof shall in no wise be shut by day (for there shall be no night there): and they shall bring the glory and the honor of the nations into it." The New Jerusalem will thus fulfil the dream of the old earthly Jerusalem whose prophets longed to see the glory of the Gentiles brought to her. The knowledge of this universal character of the heavenly city should have more influence in our day in bringing justice to all peoples. God makes no discrimination between men on the basis of color or nationality; there will be no distinction between nations and colors in the life beyond death. This picture reflects the mind of God; it should have greater influence toward an acceptance of the whole Christian ethic which contains the commandment, "Thou shalt love thy neighbor as thyself."

4. *The New Jerusalem is perfect in its holiness.*—Again John emphasizes the ethic of the gospel and its relation to the life everlasting. Nothing tainted by sin can be brought into this city: "and there shall in no wise enter into it anything unclean, or he that maketh an abomination and a lie: but only they that are written in the Lamb's book of life."

5. *The New Jerusalem is the city of perfect life.*—"And he showed me a river of water of life, bright as crystal, proceeding out of the throne of God and of the Lamb, in the midst of the street thereof. And on this side of the river and on that was the tree of life, bearing twelve manner of fruits, yielding its fruit every month: and the leaves of the tree were for the healing of the nations." The background of this beautiful symbolism is the description of the garden of Eden in

213

Genesis 2:8–10 and the vision in Ezekiel 47:1–12. The "tree of life" was in the midst of the garden of Eden, and "a river went out of Eden to water the garden." In Ezekiel's vision a stream issues from under the Temple and proceeds eastward, becoming a river too deep to be forded. The river flows on to the Dead Sea, which it converts into fresh water. On the banks of Ezekiel's river grow fruit trees which bear throughout the year. The river of the New Jerusalem issues out of the throne of God and of the Lamb. Upon its banks grows the tree of life with leaves that are "for the healing of the nations." The symbolism gives a picture of the heavenly city as the source of life everlasting. The tree of life in the garden of Eden of Genesis has become in this last book of the Bible the tree of everlasting life in the City of God. In this city is the fountainhead of all life. In it there can be no death.

6. *The New Jerusalem is the city of perfect light.*—"And there shall be night no more; and they need no light of lamp, neither light of sun; for the Lord God shall give them light." Light is the symbol of knowledge. Perhaps we may think of the light of God here as symbolizing his knowledge and his truth that shines forth from his person to give perfect knowledge to his people. In the New Jerusalem we shall know all mysteries and come to a complete understanding of the truth.

7. *The New Jerusalem is the city of perfect dominion.*—The great theme of Revelation, as we have seen again and again, is the reign or sovereignty of God in Christ. The great proclamation of the seventh angel after the breaking of the seventh seal was: "The sovereignty over the world became our Lord's and his Christ's, and he shall reign for ever and ever" (11:15). John saw the martyrs and the saints reigning with Christ for a thousand years (20:4–5). How fitting, then, that the final words of the Great Drama of the Sovereignty of God should be of the everlasting reign of God and his people: "And there shall be night no more; and they need no light of lamp, neither light of sun; for the Lord God shall give them light: and they shall reign for ever and ever."

AND THEY SHALL REIGN FOR EVER AND EVER!

214

EPILOGUE

22:6–21

†

Epilogue

CONCLUSION OF THE BOOK

(Chapter 22:6–21)

JOHN has told his story. The Great Drama of the Sovereignty of God has been written. The Seer of Patmos has recorded the great vision that came to him under the inspiration of the Holy Spirit. Now he visualizes the roll he has written as in the hands of a messenger and on its way to the churches of the Province of Asia. There are words of explanation, warning, and exhortation that yet need to be said. These he will append to his book ere he delivers it to the hand of the messenger who will speed it on its way to the churches.

Validation of the Vision.—22:6–9

John is anxious that his readers shall know that his book is authentic and that his vision is validated in the experience of a true prophet of God. He identifies himself with all other Christian prophets as if to appeal to them to recognize in his book the utterances of one whose spirit they may readily recognize as the spirit of a prophet. It is Jesus who speaks to him through the angel, saying: "These words are faithful and true: and the Lord, the God of the spirits of the prophets, sent unto his angel to show unto his servants the things which must shortly come to pass. And behold, I come quickly. Blessed is he that keepeth the words of the prophecy of this book."

The expression, "Behold, I come quickly," occurs in two

other places of this Epilogue, in 22:12 and 22:20. Undoubtedly the words in this context are an echo of the hope and expectancy of the early church with respect to the Parousia or second advent of Christ. The words occur in 2:16, but it was shown in the discussion of the letter to the church at Pergamum that the expression need not be taken there as a prediction of the Parousia. In 3:11 it is possible that the words apply to the Parousia, though this cannot be said with certainty. However, in this closing portion of the book there can be little question that the expression is a reference to the second advent. As John sends his book to the churches, he wishes to leave them with this watchword ringing in their ears. Christ was always at the doors, as it were; he had taught his disciples to be prepared for his return at any time; he had warned them to live in knowledge that his Parousia in their lifetime was always a possibility.

We should remember that "I come quickly" need not mean "I come soon," though this meaning is possible. The expression may mean, as has been pointed out, "I come suddenly." It was the unexpectedness of his return that Jesus emphasized, and not its immediacy. "I come suddenly," as a translation of this watchword, would therefore be in keeping with the emphasis of Jesus. Added to this emphasis was his constant appeal that his disciples be prepared for his return, and that is the note that is struck in the use of the watchword in this closing passage of Revelation.

In 22:20 the Seer himself answers this watchword with the words, "Amen: come, Lord Jesus." This response of the Seer is expressive of the hope and gladness with which the early Christians were taught to look for the return of the Lord. The words reflect the wholesome eschatological expectation transmitted from the early days of Christianity to the churches of the latter part of the first century. But they do not reveal an abnormal concern about eschatological matters on the part of these churches or of John. Nor do they prove that John entertained the chiliastic notions that were held by Papias. Again, the repetition of this watchword does not show that

John expected the return of Christ in his own time or that
he wrote his book as a prophecy of the events that were to
take place with the Parousia. As has been suggested, John
probably purposely refused to locate or describe the Parousia
at a particular point in his book, unless, indeed, the vision of
the Son of man on the white cloud in 14:14–16 is intended to
be a vision of Christ in his second advent. But in this instance,
if this be a vision of Christ in his Parousia, it is proleptic of
that which is to be brought from the indefinite future into the
present for purposes of teaching and not with the intent of
fixing the coming in a chronological scheme. (If we were
pressed to indicate that point at which the Parousia would
most naturally come in John's drama, had he chosen to include it as a vision, we should select that point where John
describes the final overthrow of Satan with the words, "and
fire came down from heaven and devoured them" (20:9).)

We leave this particular subject with the restatement of
that which has been said: There is here revealed a wholesome, glad expectancy of the Lord's return; and such a wholesome, glad expectancy is becoming in the life of the churches
of Christ at all times.

John is anxious for those of the Christian prophets who
read his book to think of him as one of their comrades. When
he would have worshiped the angel who was the agent
through whom he received the revelations, he is restrained,
and is told: "I am a fellow servant with thee and with thy
brethren the prophets, and with them that keep the words of
this book: worship God." John is happy to pass these words
on to his readers. Not only do they identify him as a comrade
with the Christian prophets in the Asian churches, but they
also show him to be one in spirit and service with all who
obey the truth of his book.

Warning to Heed the Message of the Book.—22:10–20

Contrary to the command that Daniel had received to
"shut up the words, and seal the book" (Daniel 12:4), John

is told, "Seal not up the words of the prophecy of this book; for the time is at hand." By this John means that his prophecy is relevant to the time in which it appears and is to be studied and applied. The angel continues: "He that is unrighteous, let him do unrighteousness still [or, yet more]: and he that is filthy, let him be made filthy still [or, yet more]: and he that is righteous, let him do righteousness still [or, yet more]: and he that is holy, let him be made holy still [or, yet more]." These are difficult words to explain. A possible interpretation is that the author means that the time is at hand for the application of the prophecies and words of his book; the book is not to be sealed but opened; now, then, in the light of the revelation of the book, the unrighteous person is to be seen as yet more unrighteous, the filthy person as yet more filthy, the righteous person as yet more righteous, the holy person as yet more holy. On the other hand, the words may emphasize the imminence of judgment in the present situation. Certainly John would not teach that the time of repentance had passed; there are places in his book which imply that even the enemies of God might repent as they faced the coming wrath of God (9:20 f.; 14:7; 16:9); and yet, the very statement "they repented not" indicates the hardness of men's hearts that leads them to persist in their sin to the bitter end. So in these words in 22:11 we may have a repetition of this suggestion of man's tendency to be what he has always been as he faces crisis or the wrath of God. In this instance the principle is applied to the righteous as well: "he that is righteous, let him do righteousness still [or, yet more]." Thus are the urgency of the crisis and the impending judgment of God emphasized by John.

John impresses upon his readers in this final appeal the importance of giving heed to the contents of his book by an emphasis upon the authority of Christ, whom he conceives to be actually the author of his writing. He is now for the first time "the Alpha and the Omega." Heretofore (in 1:8) this grand title has been reserved for the Almighty. Now, in the light of the revelation of the incarnation and Christ's exaltation to the right hand of God, John applies to Christ the name, "the Alpha and the Omega" (the first and last letters of the Greek alphabet). The great title identifies Christ more completely with God and emphasizes the all-comprehensiveness of his redemptive work. Again, John presents Christ as the Messiah, the son of David: "I am the root and the offspring of David, the bright, the morning star." As Messiah he is the most lustrous of all the sons of men.

One final repetition of the great emphasis of Revelation upon holy living is given in this closing passage. There is a promise of blessing for them that "wash their robes, that they may have the right *to come* to the tree of life, and may enter in by the gates of the city." But there is this warning for the wicked: "Without are the dogs, and the sorcerers, and the fornicators, and the murderers, and the idolaters, and every one that loveth and maketh a lie."

This closing passage contains a compelling invitation to all to accept the gospel. The Holy Spirit and the church join with Christ in this gracious invitation: "And the Spirit and the bride say, Come. And he that heareth, let him say, Come. And he that is athirst, let him come: he that will, let him take the water of life freely." The words are eloquently expressive of the great grace of God. They promise that all may have the water of life. Even those who persecute God's people may accept this call to the fountains of life in Christ. All who have drunk of the water of life are to join in this grand invitation from Christ, the Spirit, and the bride, who is the church: "And he that heareth, let him say, Come."

John wishes no one to tamper with his book or to alter its words. He is conscious that he is the spokesman of Jesus. More than any other writer of New Testament books, he reveals a consciousness of the fact that he is the author of Scripture. This is revealed in the warning: "I testify unto every man that heareth the words of the prophecy of this book, If any man shall add unto them, God shall add unto him the plagues which are written in this book: and if any man shall take away from the words of the book of this prophecy, God shall take away his part from the tree of life, and out of the holy city, which are written in this book." It would appear that the Seer intended to number any person who refused to accept his book as truth as among the enemies of Christ, or even as in the camp of those who received the mark of the beast, for any man dishonoring the book by adding to it, according to the warning, would suffer the plagues to be sent upon the enemies of God. For modern interpreters who treat the book lightly or who "add to" or "take from" it, the warning might well have meaning. At least it should serve as a caution to all who undertake to interpret it to approach the task of discovering its meaning with humility and to execute the task in travail and faithfulness.

Again there is the warning of the Christ who stands ever ready to come again to his world: "He who testifieth these things saith, Yea: I come quickly." The Seer responds joyously: "Amen, come, Lord Jesus." Thus does he voice that response that should be the church's glad reply to her Lord in any age.

Benediction.—22:21

"The grace of the Lord Jesus be with the saints. Amen."

And may we who labor for Christ in this day, far removed from the time in which these words came from the heart and mind of a great Seer, say with him and those who suffered and hoped in his day, "Amen."

BIBLIOGRAPHY

Commentaries

BECKWITH, ISBON T., *The Apocalypse of John*. New York: The Macmillan Company, 1919.

CHARLES, R. H., *A Critical and Exegetical Commentary on the Revelation of St. John*. Two Volumes. In the *International Critical Commentary*. New York: Charles Scribner's Sons, 1920.

KIDDLE, MARTIN, *The Revelation of St. John*. In the *Moffatt New Testament Commentary*. London: Hodder and Stoughton, 1940.

LENSKI, R. C. H., *The Interpretation of St. John's Revelation*. Columbus, Ohio: Lutheran Book Concern, 1935.

MOFFATT, JAMES, *The Revelation of St. John the Divine*. In the *Expositor's Greek Testament*. Grand Rapids: Wm. B. Eerdmans Publishing Company.

PEAKE, ARTHUR S., *The Revelation of St. John*. London: The Holborn Press.

SWETE, HENRY BARCLAY, *The Apocalypse of St. John*. London: Macmillan and Company, 1906.

Books on Revelation

ALLEN, CADY H., *The Message of the Book of Revelation*. New York: Abingdon-Cokesbury Press, 1939.

CARRINGTON, PHILIP, *The Meaning of the Revelation*. London: Society for Promoting Christian Knowledge, 1931.

DANA, H. E., *The Epistles and Apocalypse of John*. Dallas: Baptist Book Store, 1937.

MAURO, PHILIP, *The Patmos Vision, A Study of the Apocalypse*. Boston: Hamilton Brothers, 1925.

RAMSAY, WILLIAM H., *The Letters to the Seven Churches of Asia*. London: Hodder and Stoughton, 1904.

RICHARDSON, W. DONALD, *The Revelation of Jesus Christ*. Richmond, Va.: John Knox Press, 1939.

SCHONFIELD, HUGH J., *Saints Against Caesar*. London: Macdonald and Company, 1948.

SCOTT, C. ANDERSON, *The Book of Revelation*. London: Hodder and Stoughton, 1905.

SCOTT, E. F., *The Book of Revelation*. New York: Charles Scribner's Sons, 1940.

Books on the Apocalyptic Writings

CHARLES, R. H., *Apocrypha and Pseudepigrapha of the Old Testament*. Two Volumes. Oxford: the Clarendon Press, 1913.

CHARLES, R. H., *Eschatology, Hebrew, Jewish and Christian* (A Critical History of the Doctrine of a Future Life). London: Adam and Charles Black, 1913.

OESTERLEY, W. O. E., An *Introduction to the Books of the Apocrypha*. London: Society for Promoting Christian Knowledge, 1946.

PFEIFFER, ROBERT H., *History of New Testament Times With an Introduction to the Apocrypha*. New York: Harper and Brothers, 1949.

ROWLEY, H. H., *The Relevance of Apocalyptic, A Study of Jewish and Christian Apocalypses from Daniel to Revelation*. London: Lutterworth Press, 1944.

TORREY, CHARLES CUTLER, *The Apocryphal Literature*. New Haven: Yale University Press, 1945.